JOSHI.

Ganesh.

Book-keeping

STAGE I

Book-keeping

STAGE I

A. J. Favell, B.Sc. (Econ.)

FOURTH EDITION

D. M. Clifford, B.A., A.C.I.S., A.M.B.I.M.

Lecturer in Accounts at Tottenham Technical College

PITMAN PUBLISHING

Fourth edition 1973
Reprinted 1974

SIR ISAAC PITMAN AND SONS LTD.
Pitman House, Parker Street, Kingsway, London WC2B 5PB
P.O. Box 46038, Banda Street, Nairobi, Kenya

SIR ISAAC PITMAN (AUST.) PTY. LTD.
Pitman House, 158 Bouverie Street, Carlton, Victoria 3053, Australia

PITMAN PUBLISHING CORPORATION
6 East 43rd Street, New York, N.Y. 10017, U.S.A.

SIR ISAAC PITMAN (CANADA) LTD.
495 Wellington Street West, Toronto 135, Canada

THE COPP CLARK PUBLISHING COMPANY
517 Wellington Street West, Toronto 135, Canada

ISBN: 0 273 00374 7

Text set in 10/11pt. Monotype Times New Roman, printed by letterpress,
and bound in Great Britain at The Pitman Press, Bath

(B6217:46)

PREFACE

DEMAND for this book has been gratifyingly consistent over the years, and revision is now called for to bring it into line with current practice. Alterations have been made in the layout and format of some accounts and journals and the chapters dealing with banking and bank accounts now reflect the banks' use of computers.

The questions at the conclusion of each chapter can be supplemented by the exercises in *Graded Book-keeping Exercises*.

The permission to use past examination papers is kindly acknowledged.

Hertford
May, 1973

D.M.C.

CONTENTS

CHAPTER I

THE LEDGER AND THE CASH ACCOUNT

THE average business man has so many matters to attend to and his transactions are so numerous that it is obviously impossible for him even to attempt to remember everything that happens. For this reason he considers a written record essential to the proper conduct of his affairs and engages clerks to make permanent records of his correspondence, his purchases and sales and cash dealings. Book-keeping is the name given to the record of the transactions which involve the transfer of money or money's worth to or from the business. The primary value of any record is that it is available for ready reference when required. Therefore, if the record is properly kept, it should be possible to find immediately how the firm stands in relation to its customers, what is owed *to* the firm and what is owed *by* the firm. Further, it should show the purchases and sales made during a period of trading and from these figures, after taking into consideration the expenses paid or incurred, it should be possible to ascertain the profit made during that period.

This is sufficient, for the present, to indicate the purpose of book-keeping. The need for it is clear the moment one appreciates from experience the tremendous number of dealings in business houses today. Not every trader, however, keeps his records in exactly similar form. There is more or less general agreement on the rules to be followed, but a trader adapts these rules to the special needs of his particular business. The student, making his first acquaintance with the subject, is instructed in the general rules or principles and may thereafter proceed to study their application to the requirements of particular types of businesses.

This set of generally-accepted rules is known as the system

of *Double-entry Book-keeping*. In its simplest form this system requires two books for its operation—the Journal and the Ledger.

The Journal is ruled as follows—

Date	Particulars	Folio	£	£

The Ledger is ruled thus—

Date	Particulars	Folio	£	Date	Particulars	Folio	£

As the Ledger is the more important book, and essential to the operation of the system, it is dealt with first. The Journal is considered in a later chapter.

The Ledger

Note that a Ledger sheet is divided into two halves. The left-hand side, known as the *debit* side, and the right-hand side, known as the *credit* side, are both ruled in the same way. Each side of the Ledger sheet has a narrow column on the extreme left for the date; a wider column next to it for the particulars of each transaction; next a narrow column headed "Folio" for reference purposes; and, finally, on the extreme right of each side is the money column ruled for £ and p. In the past, Ledger sheets ruled in this way were bound together in a volume known as the *Ledger*. Even today there are many small businesses in which all book-keeping is completed by hand and Ledgers ruled in this way are used. Each sheet (or *folio*) of the Ledger is numbered and contains an *account*. There is a separate *account* for each aspect of the affairs of the business. Thus all cash transactions are recorded in the Cash Account; the sale of goods is shown in the Sales Account; the payment of wages appears in the Wages Account and so on.

Today large businesses and many not so large businesses use accounting machines; much of the routine book-keeping, including completion of the Ledger accounts, is done by machinery. Of course, office workers are still needed to operate these machines but in such businesses the labour of writing accounts by hand is no longer necessary. In a mechanized accounts office the Ledger sheets cannot be bound together since a Ledger sheet must be inserted in the machine when an entry is to be made. Loose-leaf Ledger sheets which are ruled in a slightly different way are used and these are filed in steel trays or boxes. At this stage, however, we are concerned with the principles of book-keeping and variations in the details of presentation can be considered at a later stage.

The double-entry system involves the recording in the Ledger of the *two* aspects of every transaction. If goods are bought for cash two things happen to the buyer which he records in his books, and two things happen to the seller, which *he* records in *his* books. The buyer has parted with or "lost" money and has received or "gained" goods: the seller has parted with or "lost" goods and "gained" money. The buyer will therefore record in his Cash Account the "loss" of money by *crediting* that account (entering on the right-hand side) and record in his Goods Received Account on the *debit* side that goods were received. The seller in *his* books will *debit* his Cash Account showing money received and *credit* his Goods Sold Account, showing goods parted with.

Here, then, is a fundamental rule. Whenever a debit is made in one account a corresponding credit must be made in another account.

Cash Account

To enable the beginner to become better acquainted with the form an account takes in the Ledger, it would not be out of place at this point to prepare a Cash Account. Such an account is a record of money received and money paid away, and is necessary not only for reference purposes but as a check on the amount of money in the firm's till or cash box. Without a separate record, it would not be possible to say whether the cash in hand at the close of business for the day is the correct sum or not, as it merely represents the difference between the cash placed in the till and the amounts taken out. But we may assume the sum to be correct if it agrees with what the written record of cash takings and payments shows it should be.

Example 1

Enter the following transactions in the Cash Account (the second item *is* to be entered even though it should be dealt with in a Petty Cash Account)—

			£
Jan.	1.	Sold furniture for cash	30·00
	2.	Bought postage stamps	0·50
	3.	Bought for cash two tables	9·00
	7.	Cash sales this week	18·60
	12.	Purchased stationery for cash	1·50
	14.	Sold goods for cash	17·00
	19.	Bought sundry articles for cash	26·70
	21.	Cash sales	19·80
	24.	T. Smith paid us his account	12·00
	28.	Paid salary to assistant	24·00
	29.	Cash sales to date	22·00
	31.	Paid electric light account	5·00

Dr. CASH ACCOUNT *Cr.*

Date	Particulars	Fol.	Amount	Date	Particulars	Fol.	Amount
19..			£	19..			£
Jan. 1	To Sales . .		30·00	Jan. 2	By Postage Stamps		0·50
7	,, Sales . .		18·60	3	,, Purchases .		9·00
14	,, Sales . .		17·00	12	,, Stationery .		1·50
21	,, Sales . .		19·80	19	,, Purchases .		26·70
24	,, T. Smith .		12·00	28	,, Salary .		24·00
29	,, Sales . .		22·00	31	,, Electric Light .		5·00
					,, Balance . .	c/d	52·70
			£119·40				£119·40
Feb. 1	To Balance .	b/d	52·70				

Now if the above Cash Account is carefully examined it should be observed that—

1. The left-hand half is headed by the abbreviation *Dr.* and the right-hand half by the abbreviation *Cr.* *Dr.* stands for Debtor and *Cr.* for Creditor. The left-hand half is called the *debit* side of the Cash Account, and the right-hand half is called the *credit* side.

2. The items as entered on the debit (or left-hand half) of the account are prefaced by the word "To." The items on the credit side are prefaced by the word "By." In other words the Cash Account is debtor *to* the items on the left-hand side, and is creditor *by* the items on the other side. We speak of debiting a Ledger account when we enter an item in the left half, and of crediting the Ledger account when we enter an item in the right half. The practice of writing the words "To" and "By" is a matter of convention and many book-keepers now regard this as an unnecessary labour. Therefore in the illustrations shown in the remainder of this book the prefixes "To" and "By" will not be used.

3. The items on the debit side all represent money received whereas the items on the credit side represent money paid out. This is an example of a rule in book-keeping. All money received is debited (i.e. entered on the debit or left side) to the Cash Account, and all payments made in cash are credited to the account. The Cash Account, therefore, is a record of

dealings with the business cash, and it is obvious that if we want to know how much cash remains in the cash box at the end of the month we must subtract the total of the payments from the total receipts. On separate paper, not in the Ledger, we can note that the credit side amounts to £66·70, and the debit side to £119·40. The difference between these sums is £52·70, which means that, after making payments to the extent of £66·70 from the money received during January, there remains in hand the sum of £52·70. This should be the total of cash in the cash box or till.

The amount of cash remaining appears on the credit side of the Cash Account against the wording "By Balance." Having entered this sum the two sides of the account are added and the totals inserted. The totals should agree and should be written level with each other even though one side may contain very few items as compared with the other. We call this the balancing and closing of the Cash Account. We have ascertained the cash in hand at the end of January, but that amount is the cash in hand with which we shall commence business on 1st February. This explains why the balance in hand as shown on the credit side of the January account is "carried down" to the February account. We are justified in placing it on the debit side of the new account as received, though it be but part remaining of the receipts during the preceding month. Apart from the balance brought down from the account for the preceding month, the new Cash Account will follow on the lines of that already prepared. The receipts will be entered on the debit side and the payments on the credit side, as in the example below wherein the above account for January is continued for a further period.

Example 2

		£
Feb. 1.	Cash in hand	52·70
2.	Received from J. Jones in payment of his account .	18·00
4.	Bought goods for cash	31·50
6.	Paid carriage on purchases	2·00
7.	Paid sundry expenses	2·22

| Dr. | | | | CASH ACCOUNT | | | Cr. |

Date	Particulars	Fol.	Amount	Date	Particulars	Fol.	Amount
19.. Feb. 1 2	Balance . . J. Jones . .	b/d	£ 52·70 18·00 £70·70	19.. Feb. 4 6 7	Purchases . . Carriage . . Sundry expenses Balance .	c/d	£ 31·50 2·00 2·22 34·98 £70·70
Feb. 8	Balance . .	b/d	34·98				

In this instance the account has been balanced at a date other than at the end of the month.

In addition to the value of the Cash Account as a record of receipts and payments, it enables the trader to ascertain the cash in hand at any time without counting over the actual coins and notes in the cash box.

EXERCISE 1

Enter the following transactions in the Cash Account—

		£
Jan.	1. Sold goods for cash	37·50
	2. Bought packing material	2·52
	3. Bought postage stamps	1·00
	4. Paid travelling expenses	0·75
	5. Sold goods for cash	12·20
	6. Paid cash for goods bought today . . .	18·00
	7. Paid wages to assistant	6·00
	(Cash balance, £21·43)	

EXERCISE 2

Enter the following transactions in the Cash Account—

		£
Jan.	1. Sold goods for cash	20·00
	6. Bought goods for cash	12·00
	9. Paid cash for wrapping paper	3·00
	14. Cash sales to this date	23·50
	19. Received cash from F. Smith in payment of his account	16·22
	25. Paid electric light account	6·00
	27. Cash sales	19·56
	31. Paid one month's rent	10·50

Balance the account and carry down the balance for Exercise 3.

EXERCISE 3

Carry on the Cash Account for the month of February—

		£
Feb.	1. Balance in hand from last month	47·78
	Paid assistant's salary in cash	12·00
	4. Sales to this date for cash	18·62
	12. Bought new scales for shop	24·00
	14. P. Jackson paid amount owing for goods supplied	31·00
	17. Received from B. McKenna on account of amount owing	8·20
	24. Bought goods for cash	27·50
	26. Paid gasfitter for repairs	1·20
	28. Paid one month's rent	10·50

Balance the accounts and carry down the balance for Exercise 4.

EXERCISE 4

Carry on the Cash Account for the month of March—

		£
Mar.	1. Balance in hand from last month	30·40
	2. Paid assistant's salary in cash	12·00
	10. Bought electric light fittings	4·50
	14. Received from B. McKenna balance of amount due	10·00
	19. Sold goods for cash	22·70
	26. Bought goods for cash	30·00
	27. Received cash from P. Thomas for goods supplied	6·37
	31. Paid one month's rent	10·50

Balance the account as at 31st March and carry down the balance.

(Cash balance, £12·47)

ADDITIONAL EXERCISES

Graded Book-keeping Exercises, Nos. 1, 2, and 3.

CHAPTER II

DOUBLE-ENTRY AND CAPITAL

THE double-entry system explained in the previous chapter can now be illustrated by means of the following example—

Example

		£
July 1.	M. A. Stubbs commenced business with cash	60·00
3.	Bought for cash, goods	40·00
4.	Sold for cash, goods	70·00
6.	Lent T. Benson	10·00
7.	Paid carriage on goods purchased	3·50
9.	T. Benson repaid on account	5·00

Capital

The value (usually, in the first place, cash) which a man invests in his business is termed his capital. He takes it from his personal cash and treats it as belonging to the business and no longer available for private purposes. His private and business affairs are separate and in book-keeping we regard them as distinct. The accounts are the accounts of the business and we treat the owner as separate from the business. He puts capital into it and that capital is owing by the business to him.

The entries for the first transaction above are—

Debit Cash Account, £60, as the business receives that sum from the owner.

Credit a new Ledger account called Capital Account, £60, treating the Capital Account as the personal account of the owner, and thus we record that he has parted with £60 to the business. These are the entries required to record the two aspects of the first transaction.

July 3. On buying goods for cash, the cash is paid out, but in place of it the business receives the goods.

We could, if we wished, enter four aspects of this transaction. The business spends £40 and the seller of the goods receives that sum. The seller parts with goods value £40 which the business receives. But as cash is paid there is seldom the need to record to whom it is paid as its equivalent in goods is at once received. Instead, Cash Account is credited as the money is spent and a new account headed "Purchases" is opened and debited. This account will contain, eventually, all the purchases made by the trader of goods bought for sale.

July 4. A sale of goods for cash necessarily involves the receipt of cash by the business and the sending away of goods. These are the two aspects to be entered for this item. The Cash Account is debited with the £70 received, and a new account, headed "Sales," is opened in which are entered on the credit side this and all other sales during the period.

July 6. A loan of £10 to T. Benson implies that the business handed over £10 from its cash and that Benson received it. The Cash Account is credited and an account headed "T. Benson" is debited to record that he received that sum. This is an example of a personal account, one relating to a person, which it is necessary to open in order that it may be seen at a glance how the business stands in relation to these persons.

July 9. On T. Benson repaying £5, the business receives the cash and Benson pays it. Cash Account is debited with £5 and T. Benson's account is credited. The difference between the two sides of his account is the amount he still owes.

July 7. The payment of expenses of any kind, e.g. wages, stationery, rent, rates, travelling expenses, involves a credit entry in the Cash Account as the money is spent, but this type of payment, it should be noted, represents a loss to the business. An account is opened for each different type of expense, so that the owner can see clearly and exactly how money has been spent.

These items will appear in the Ledger as below—

Dr.			CASH ACCOUNT (1)				Cr.
19.. July 1 4 9	Capital Sales. T. Benson	. L.2 . L.4 . L.5	£ 60·00 70·00 5·00	19.. July 3 6 7	Purchases T. Benson Carriage	. L.3 . L.5 . L.6	£ 40·00 10·00 3·50

Dr.			CAPITAL (2)				Cr.
			£	19.. July 1	Cash .	. L.1	£ 60·00

Dr.			PURCHASES (3)				Cr.
19.. July 3	Cash .	. L.1	£ 40·00				£

Dr.			SALES (4)				Cr.
			£	19.. July 4	Cash .	. L.1	£ 70·00

Dr.			T. BENSON (Loan to) (5)				Cr.
19.. July 6	Cash .	. L.1	£ 10·00	19.. July 9	Cash .	. L.1	£ 5·00

Dr.			CARRIAGE (6)				Cr.
19.. July 7	Cash .	. L.1	£ 3·50				£

The reader may have observed from this example that the recording of the two aspects of a transaction involves every debit entry having a corresponding credit entry. As mentioned earlier, it is a rule of double-entry book-keeping that this should be so in the Ledger accounts, and the closest attention must be given to ensure that this rule is carried out.

Ledger Folios

The pages of the Ledger (and of all the books mentioned in subsequent chapters) are numbered for reference purposes. The term "folio" refers to a page of the Ledger and the page numbers are called "folio numbers." In practice, when making an entry, a note is made in the folio column of the page or book where the other entry appears. Not only does this provide a reference number for the second entry, but by making it a rule to enter the folio number when the item is being posted it provides a check that the double-entry has been made.

To enable students to get used to using folio numbers right from the start it will be found convenient (in spite of having to put many accounts, when working exercises, on one page) to number each account consecutively as if on a separate page and to enter these numbers in the appropriate folio columns against entries, but prefixed by the initial letter of the book, e.g. "L" for Ledger, "CB" for Cash Book, and "J" for Journal. At a later stage, subdivisions of the Ledger and Journal will require distinctive initials like "GL" for General Ledger and "BJ" for "Bought Journal."

Thus in the accounts shown on p. 11, the credit for the first debit appearing in the Cash Account appears in the Capital Account, on p. 2, so the folio for that debit is entered as "L.2." The folio in the Capital Account is given as "L.1" since the debit is on p. 1 in the Cash Account.

If all the folios given in that example are followed through with care the treatment of folio numbers in all subsequent exercises should be perfectly clear.

EXERCISE 5

Record the following transactions in double-entry form in A. Bede's Ledger—

			£
Jan.	1. A. Bede commenced business with capital in cash	.	100·00
	4. Bought sundry articles for cash .	. . . .	80·00
	7. Paid carriage on goods bought .	. . . .	2·00
	10. Sold goods for cash .	. . . .	47·50
	14. Cash sales	. . . .	21·00
	17. Paid for cleaning of shop .	. . . .	0·75
	24. Sales to this date for cash .	. . . .	11·00
	27. Bought for cash, goods	. . . .	18·71
	31. Paid for postage stamps .	. . . .	0·25

Balance the Cash Account as on 31st January and carry down the balance. Do not balance the other accounts for the present.

(Cash balance, £77·79)

EXERCISE 6

Treat as Exercise 5.

			£
Dec.	1. J. Fuller commenced business as a provision dealer with capital in cash	. . . .	200·00
	6. Bought provisions for cash	. . . .	180·75
	12. Sold provisions for cash .	. . . .	86·75
	14. Lent to B. Fuller in cash .	. . . .	20·00
	15. Sold provisions for cash .	. . . .	170·50
	18. Bought provisions for cash	. . . .	25·00
	21. Sold provisions for cash .	. . . .	43·33
	28. Paid travelling expenses in cash .	. . . .	10·00
	29. B. Fuller repaid on account	. . . .	10·00
	30. Paid wages in cash .	. . . .	8·00
	31. Paid rent in cash .	. . . .	12·00

Balance the Cash Account as at 31st December and carry down the balance.

(Cash balance, £254·83)

EXERCISE 7

Treat as Exercise 6.

			£
July	1. D. Thomson commenced to deal in second-hand motorcars with capital in cash of .	. . .	240·00
	5. Bought four second-hand cars for	. . .	180·00
	7. Paid haulage expenses in cash .	. . .	5·00
	9. Sold car for cash .	. . . .	45·00
	15. Sold car for cash .	. . . .	80·00
	20. Sold a third car for cash .	. . . .	75·00
	23. Bought another car for cash	. . . .	60·00
	24. Sold fourth car for cash .	. . . .	50·00
	30. Paid assistant in cash .	. . . .	10·00

Balance the Cash Account as at 30th July and carry down the balance.

(Cash balance, £235·00)

ADDITIONAL EXERCISES

Graded Book-keeping Exercises, Nos. 4, 5, and 8

CHAPTER III

THE TRIAL BALANCE

IN practice many thousands of entries will be made in the Ledger in the course of the business year. Accuracy is essential but errors may creep in. Periodically the book-keeper makes a check on the entries to assure himself that they are accurate before going on to prepare the final accounts (as discussed in Chapters IV and V). This check is known as the Trial Balance. It may be taken out at any time, but in working exercises the student should prepare it on Journal paper after the last transaction is entered.

The Trial Balance is based on the principle that, as every transaction appears twice in the Ledger accounts, once on the debit side and once on the credit side, the total of the debit entries must equal the total of the credit entries. Taking the example in the preceding chapter and placing in two columns the debit and credit items we should obtain the following results.

TRIAL BALANCES (TOTALS METHOD)

Account						Debit Totals	Credit Totals
						£	£
Cash .	•	•	•	•		135·00	53·50
Capital	•	•	•	•			60·00
Purchases	•	•	•	•		40·00	
Sales .	•	•	•	•			70·00
T. Benson	•	•	•	•		10·00	5·00
Carriage	•	•	•	•		3·50	
						£188·50	£188·50

Present-day practice, however, makes use of the *balances* of the accounts, not the totals. In the Cash Account shown the debit side is greater than the credit side by £81·50. This is the balance and it is placed in the debit column of the Trial Balance. Acting on the same lines with each account the Trial Balance would appear thus—

TRIAL BALANCE

	Dr.	Cr.
	£	£
Cash	81·50	
Capital		60·00
Purchases . . .	40·00	
Sales		70·00
T. Benson . . .	5·00	
Carriage . . .	3·50	
	£130·00	£130·00

This is the method the student should follow and he should experience no difficulty in preparing a Trial Balance if the following rules are borne in mind—

1. If the *debit* side of an account is the greater, place the amount by which it is greater in the *debit* column of the Trial Balance.

2. If the *credit* side is the greater, then place the amount by which it is greater in the *credit* column of the Trial Balance.

3. If the two sides agree no entry is made in the Trial Balance.

The amounts agreeing with Rule 1 are called Debit Balances; those agreeing with Rule 2 are Credit Balances, taking their names from the side which is the greater in amount.

If the Trial Balance totals agree the entries in the Ledger may be taken as correct, but it is not a positive proof of accurate book-keeping. The two columns may agree in total notwithstanding that errors of the following kinds may have been made—

1. An item omitted completely (no debit entry, no credit entry).

2. A transaction entered on both sides but in the wrong account or accounts.

3. "Compensating" errors—where the error (or errors) on one side is offset by an equal amount of error or errors on the other.

But the Trial Balance totals will not agree if an item has been posted twice on one side of the Ledger or if the double-entry has not been completed, and it then becomes necessary to trace the error in order that the accounts may be corrected (see Chapter XXIV).

A Trial Balance can be defined as a list of balances extracted from the Ledger as at a certain date.

EXERCISE 8

Enter the following transactions in double-entry form in the Ledger and check your work by taking out a Trial Balance—

		£
Mar. 1.	Thomas Swanwick commenced business as nurseryman with capital in cash	50·00
2.	His brother, Frederick, lent him in cash	100·00
3.	Bought fruit trees for cash	50·00
7.	Bought rose trees for cash	40·00
8.	Sold rose and fruit trees for cash	30·00
10.	Paid cash for coal and coke for greenhouses	7·00
14.	Cash sales of trees	36·00
18.	Paid carriage	3·00
24.	Sold trees for cash	25·00
27.	Repaid to brother £50 on account of loan	50·00

(Trial Balance totals, £191)

EXERCISE 9

Treat as Exercise 8.

Dec. 1. S. Williams began to deal in wireless sets, with capital in cash of £80.
3. Bought six "Wideworld" sets at £10 each and paid cash.
7. Sold two sets for cash at £15·75 each.
12. Paid sundry expenses, £0·50.
19. Sold further two sets for cash at £15·75 each.
21. Customer who bought a set on 19th inst. returned it as unsuitable. Refunded cash, £15·75.
29. Sold three sets for cash at £15·75 each.
31. Paid commission to assistant, £1·50.

(Trial Balance totals, £190·25)

ADDITIONAL EXERCISES

Graded Book-keeping Exercises, Nos. 6 and 9.

CHAPTER IV

THE TRADING AND PROFIT AND LOSS ACCOUNT, STOCK, AND DRAWINGS

THE aim of all businesses is to make profits. A businessman will therefore be anxious to discover whether his business has made a profit and, if so, how much. First he will wish to calculate his *gross profit:* the difference between the total cost of the goods he has purchased and the amount he has obtained by selling them. To buy an article for £10 and to sell it for £15 is to realize a gross profit of £5, but if the expenses incurred in selling it amount to £2, the net gain coming to the trader is but £3. The latter is known as the net profit and may be defined as the amount by which the gross profit exceeds the expenses of selling and of running the business establishment.

The gross profit is found by preparing a Trading Account. The Profit and Loss Account is used for ascertaining the net profit.

The Trading Account is prepared at the end of the trading period after the arithmetical accuracy of the books has been proved by extracting the Trial Balance. The total cost of the purchases is already on record in the Purchases Account and the total sales in the Sales Account. These accounts are closed by the balances being transferred to the Trading Account which, making use of the transactions in Chapter II, appears as below—

Dr.				TRADING ACCOUNT			*Cr.*
19.. Jul. 9	Purchases	.	£ 40·00	19.. Jul. 9	Sales . . .		£ 70·00

The balance of this account, that is, the difference between the two sides, is £30 and, if all the purchases have been sold, is the gross profit.

Stock at Close

It is unusual, however, for a trader to have sold *all* his goods at a particular date. At the close of the Trading Period it is necessary to take stock to find the value of the goods remaining on hand. Stock books or sheets are used and a list made of such goods. Their value is noted at actual cost price or, if the current market price for similar goods has fallen, then at less than cost price. Assuming, in the above case, the stock on hand is worth £12 at cost price, the cost price of the goods sold (which realized £70) is £40 − £12, viz. £28. The gross profit is therefore £70 − £28 = £42.

The book-keeping entries for the stock at close are as follows—

Debit a new account headed Stock Account.

Credit the Trading Account.

Net Profit

The Trading Account is then balanced and the balance is carried down to the credit of Profit and Loss Account in order that the net profit may be ascertained. All the expenses are brought into the Profit and Loss Account so that the balance represents the net profit for the trading period. The two accounts are usually shown as two parts of one account (see p. 20), but it should be noticed, also, that the double-entry in respect of the net profit is in the trader's Capital Account.

The net profit is the result of the owner's personal efforts and is his property, and for that reason it is placed to the credit of his Capital Account along with the original capital he put into the business. The Capital Account is balanced and the balance carried down to the new period.

The following are the accounts in Chapter II as affected by the preparation of the final accounts.

Dr.   CASH ACCOUNT (1)   Cr.

19..				£	19..				£
July 1	Capital	.	L.2	60·00	July 3	Purchases	.	L.3	40·00
4	Sales	.	L.4	70·00	6	T. Benson	.	L.5	10·00
9	T. Benson	.	L.5	5·00	7	Carriage	.	L.6	3·50
					9	Balance	.	c/d	81·50
				£135·00					£135·00
Jul. 10	Balance	.	b/d	81·50					

Dr.   CAPITAL ACCOUNT (2)   Cr.

19..				£	19..				£
July 9	Balance	.	c/d	98·50	July 1	Cash	.	L.1	60·00
					9	Net Profit	.	L.7	38·50
				£98·50					£98·50
					July 10	Balance	.	b/d	98·50

Dr.   PURCHASES ACCOUNT (3)   Cr.

19..				£	19..			£
July 3	Cash	.	L.1	40·00	July 9	Transfer to Trading A/c.	L.7	40·00

Dr.   SALES ACCOUNT (4)   Cr.

19..			£	19..				£
July 9	Transfer to Trading A/c.	L.7	70·00	July 4	Cash	.	L.1	70·00

Dr.   T. BENSON (Loan to) (5)   Cr.

19..				£	19..				£
July 6	Cash	.	L.1	10·00	July 9	Cash	.	L.1	5·00
					9	Balance	.	c/d	5·00
				£10·00					£10·00
Jul. 10	Balance	.	b/d	5·00					

Dr.   CARRIAGE ACCOUNT (6)   Cr.

19..				£	19..			£
July 7	Cash	.	L.1	£3·50	July 9	Profit and Loss A/c.	.	L.7	£3·50

TRADING AND PROFIT AND LOSS ACCOUNT (7)

19..			£	19..			£
uly 9	Purchases .	. L.3	40·00	July 9	Sales . .	. L.4	70·00
	Gross Profit	. c/d	42·00		Stock. .	. L.8	12·00
			£82·00				£82·00
July 9	Carriage .	. L.6	3·50	July 9	Gross Profit	. b/d	42·00
	Net Profit						
	Transferred to						
	Capital A/c.	. L.2	38·50				
			£42·00				£42·00

Dr.		STOCK ACCOUNT (8)					Cr.
19..			£				£
July 10	Trading A/c.	. L.7	12·00				

Drawings

The owner may withdraw all or part of the profit made. This may be done at the close of the trading period or withdrawals of cash may be made during the year in anticipation of the profit to come. Such withdrawals are called "drawings." Cash Account will, of course, be credited as the cash is paid out. As the owner has received the amount, the debit entry may be made in his Capital Account, or, if there are several sums, then first in a Drawings Account, to be transferred from that account to the Capital Account at the close of the period. The following accounts have been adapted from the above to illustrate this point. The Cash Account is not shown as the credit entries are easily understood.

Dr.			DRAWINGS				Cr.
19..			£	19..			£
July 4	Cash . . .		10·00	July 31	Transfer to		
28	Cash . . .		10·00		Capital A/c. .		20·00
			£20·00				£20·00

Dr.						CAPITAL ACCOUNT			*Cr.*
19..				£	19..				£
July 31	Drawings .	.	c/d	20·00	July 1	Cash . .	.		60·00
31	Balance .	.		78·50	31	Net Profit .	.		38·50
				£98·50					£98·50
					Aug. 1	Balance .	.	b/d	78·50

If the owner should take goods from the business for his private use these are usually charged to him at cost. Purchases Account should be credited and the Drawings Account debited.

Losses

It seldom happens that a gross loss occurs in business, which would mean that the sales fetch less than the goods cost to buy. But should it occur the balance of the Trading Account would appear on the credit side and would be transferred to the debit of Profit and Loss Account. The gross loss and the expenses in this account would show a greater net loss. The balance would therefore appear on the credit side of the Profit and Loss Account and would be transferred to the debit of the Capital Account.

The Capital Account when balanced would show a smaller amount due to the owner as the loss results from his own efforts.

Though a gross loss is unusual it may occasionally happen that the expenses are greater than the gross profit, and in that case a net loss results.

Example of Gross Profit but Net Loss

Dr.						TRADING AND PROFIT AND LOSS ACCOUNT			*Cr.*
19..				£	19..				£
Dec. 31	Purchases .	.	c/d	120	Dec. 31	Sales .	.		140
	Gross Profit .	.		30		Stock at Close			10
				£150					£150
Dec. 31	Wages .	.		10	Dec. 31	Gross Profit .	.	b/d	30
	Expenses .	.		18		Net Loss .	.		3
	Carriage .	.		5					
				£33					£33

Dr.   CAPITAL ACCOUNT   *Cr.*

19.. Dec. 31	Net Loss Balance	. .	. .	c/d	£ 3 197	19.. Jul. 1	Cash .	.	.		£ 200
					£200						£200
						Jan. 1	Balance	.	.	b/d	197

EXERCISE 10

Enter the following transactions in the Ledger and, after extracting a Trial Balance, find the Gross Profit and Net Profit for the period by means of the Trading and Profit and Loss Account—

		£
Jan. 1.	J. Smith started business with cash	150·00
	Bought tea for cash	80·00
5.	Paid transport expenses	5·00
8.	Paid wages	6·00
9.	Sold tea for cash	70·00
15.	Sold tea for cash	50·00

Stock on hand at 15th January, *nil.*

(Gross Profit, £40. Net Profit, £29.)

EXERCISE 11

Treat as Exercise 10.

		£
July 1.	T. Harman commenced business with cash . . .	200·00
	Bought silk for cash	80·00
5.	Sold silk for cash	50·00
18.	Bought silk for cash	120·00
25.	Sold silk for cash	170·00
28.	Sold *remainder* of silk for cash	60·00
30.	Paid wages in cash	20·00

(Gross Profit, £80. Net Profit, £60.)

EXERCISE 12

Open the necessary Ledger accounts to record the following. Test your double-entry by taking out a Trial Balance. Find the Gross Profit and the Net Profit for the period—

		£
Jan. 1.	J. Jackson started business as furniture dealer with cash	100·00
	Bought furniture for cash	70·00
6.	Sold furniture for cash	50·00
13.	Paid transport expenses	5·00
20.	Sold furniture for cash	45·00
31.	Paid wages	15·00

Stock of goods on hand at 31st January, £20.

(Gross Profit, £45. Net Profit, £25.)

EXERCISE 13

W. Worthington started business on 1st July with cash £240, and the following were his transactions during the month of July. Enter up his Ledger accounts, take out Trial Balance, and find his Gross and Net Profit—

		£
July	1. Bought tweed for cash	200·00
	7. Sold tweed for cash	180·00
	12. Sold tweed for cash	80·00
	19. Paid wages in cash	10·00
	28. Withdrew cash for private purposes	12·00
	31. Paid sundry expenses in cash	5·00

Stock on hand at 31st July, £40.

(Gross Profit, £100. Net Profit, £85.)

ADDITIONAL EXERCISES

Graded Book-keeping Exercises, Nos. 7 and 10.

CHAPTER V

THE BALANCE SHEET

WITH the transfer of the net profit (or net loss) to the Capital Account the double-entry book-keeping for the period is completed. The Ledger contains a complete record of the transactions and the financial results have been ascertained. But the Trial Balance, which proved to a large extent the arithmetical accuracy of the books, is now no longer correct. Some balances, such as that of the Cash Account, remain the same: others, such as that of the Capital Account, have been altered, whilst many of them have been transferred to the Trading and Profit and Loss Account. All the changes that have been made (transfers to and from the Trading and Profit and Loss Account) have been done by double-entry so if a *new* list of balances were extracted from the Ledger its total of debit balances should agree with its total of credit balances, as did those of the Trial Balance.

The second list contains the remaining balances all of which will appear in the *Balance Sheet*. A list of the balances of accounts remaining at the end of the example on pp. 19 and 20 is as follows—

Account					Debit Balances	Credit Balances
					£	£
Cash .	.	.	.	.	81·50	
Capital	.	.	.	.		98·50
Benson	.	.	.	.	5·00	
Stock .	.	.	.	.	12·00	
					£98·50	£98·50

The trader, however, is usually anxious to know the exact financial position of the business as at the close of each trading period, so the Balance Sheet is set out in such a way as to make this as clear as possible. All those accounts which are left with a balance after the completion of the Trading and Profit and Loss Account are either *Real* or *Personal*, that is, those dealing with different forms of property or those recording dealings with persons, and all these accounts will fall into two groups, namely, *Assets* if they have debit balances and *Liabilities* if they have credit balances.

The Balance Sheet does not appear in the form of a Trial Balance, as illustrated on p. 24, nor is it presented in the form of an account with debit items on the left and credit balances on the right. The *Balance Sheet* is neither an account nor a Trial Balance but a statement of the financial affairs of the business drawn up on a particular day. In the case illustrated below it is 9th July. Perhaps to emphasize that the Balance Sheet is unique, the *credit* balances (Liabilities and Capital) are shown on the *left* and *debit* balances (Assets) on the *right*.

The sequence of work is—

1. Complete the Ledger entries.
2. Extract a Trial Balance (arithmetic check).
3. Complete the Trading and Profit and Loss Account (i.e. further Ledger work).
4. Prepare the Balance Sheet. This verifies as far as possible the work completed up to that time and shows the state of the financial affairs of the business on that date.

The Balance Sheet in conventional form, based on the accounts in Chapter IV, is shown below. Note that double cash ruled account paper is used. This is similar to the Journal ruled paper illustrated on p. 2.

BALANCE SHEET OF A. TRADER
AS AT 9th JULY, 19..

Liabilities	£	£	Assets	£	£
Capital . . .	60·00		T. Benson (loan) .		5·00
Add Net Profit .	38·50		Stock on hand .		12·00
		98·50	Cash in hand .		81·50
		£98·50			£98·50

Any drawings by the owner will, of course, be shown as a deduction from his Capital Account on the Balance Sheet as it is customary to show the *whole* of the contents of the Capital Account.

Of course, this simple example does not exhaust the possible forms assets and liabilities may take. Machinery, premises, trade debtors, office furniture, and fittings may be owned by a business and will appear among its assets as valuable possessions. On the other hand, sums owing to creditors comprise a usual form of liability in a business undertaking and will appear under that heading in the Balance Sheet. *Capital* is shown on the liabilities side as it has a credit balance, although some readers may find it difficult to see why capital is a liability. Can the proprietor of a business owe himself money? In fact this is perfectly possible if the business is regarded as an entity quite separate and distinct from the proprietor as a private individual. However, the heading most commonly seen on the left hand side of a Balance Sheet is "Liabilities and Capital." There is a number of ways in which a Balance Sheet can be presented but, for the present, the form of presentation shown on the previous page will be used. It is useful to note that the assets are listed in reverse order of *liquidity* (the ease with which they can be sold and thus converted into cash). The most liquid (cash itself) appears last and permanent fixed assets (such as Land and Buildings) appear first. This matter is discussed more fully in Chapter XV.

EXERCISE 14

Tom Jones, furniture dealer, started business on 10th October with £50 capital in cash. Open his Ledger and record the following transactions—

		£
Oct. 10.	Bought sundry articles of furniture for cash	35·00
12.	Paid transport expenses	2·00
14.	Sold furniture for cash	25·00
15.	Sold remainder of furniture for cash	28·00
15.	Paid odd man for assistance	2·00

Take out Trial Balance.

(Cash Balance, £64. Trial Balance totals, £103.)

Prepare final accounts (Trading and Profit and Loss Account and Balance Sheet).

(Gross Profit, £18. Net Profit, £14. Balance Sheet totals, £64.)

EXERCISE 15

J. Graham, motor dealer, started business with £400 capital in cash on 1st October. Open his Ledger accounts and record the following transactions—

		£
Oct.	2. Bought two second-hand cars for cash . . .	340·00
	3. Sold one car for cash	220·00
	4. Sold second car for cash	180·00
	Paid haulage charge in cash	2·00
	Paid assistant	10·00

Take out Trial Balance.

     (Cash Balance, £448. Trial Balance totals, £800.)

Prepare final accounts.

     (Gross Profit, £60. Net Profit, £48. Balance Sheet totals, £448.)

EXERCISE 16

J. Schubert started business with capital in cash £150 on 1st November. Open his Ledger accounts and enter the following transactions—

		£
Nov.	1. Bought for cash four pianos at £30 each . .	120·00
	3. Paid transport expenses	5·00
	4. Sold two pianos for cash at £45 each . .	90·00
	5. Sold further two pianos for cash at £45 each .	90·00
	7. Bought three second-hand pianos for cash . .	50·00
	10. Sold one piano for cash	23·00
	12. Drew cash for personal use . . .	10·00

Take out Trial Balance.

     (Cash balance, £168. Trial Balance totals, £353.)

Prepare final accounts. Value of stock on hand, £32.

     (Gross Profit, £65. Net Profit, £60. Balance Sheet totals, £200.)

EXERCISE 17

G. Phillips commenced to deal in second-hand cameras on 15th March with a capital in cash of £60. Record this and the following transactions in his Ledger—

		£
Mar.	16. Bought seven cameras for cash . . .	15·50
	18. Bought four cameras for cash . . .	7·50
	19. Bought "Studio" camera and two "Reflex" cameras for cash	35·00
	24. Sold by advertisement ten cameras for cash .	36·00
	29. Sold one "Reflex" camera for cash . .	8·40
	30. Paid cash for advertisements . . .	1·50
	31. Withdrew cash for personal use on account of Profit .	12·00

Extract a Trial Balance.

     (Cash Balance, £32·90. Trial Balance totals, £104·40.)

Prepare final accounts, taking the stock of cameras on hand as worth at cost price, £31.

     (Gross Profit, £17·40. Net Profit, £15·90. Balance Sheet totals, £63·90.)

ADDITIONAL EXERCISES

Graded Book-keeping Exercises, Nos. 7 and 10.

CHAPTER VI

CREDIT TRANSACTIONS AND PURCHASES

A TRADER may buy goods and pay cash for them at the time of purchase. Similarly he may sell goods to customers for immediate cash payment. Most of a trader's transactions, however, are on credit, that is, he is given time in which to pay and he, in turn, allows his customers to postpone payment for a period. The goods pass from buyer to seller immediately, but the "credit period" allowed may be a few days or as many months. Where the trader buys for cash, the Cash Account is credited by the amount he pays out, and in the case of a sale for cash, the Cash Account is debited with the money received. As, however, no money passes at the time of a purchase or sale *on credit*, no entry can be made in the Cash Account. Instead, a record is kept of the person to or from whom the money is due according to whether it is a purchase or sale.

Example

		£
Jan. 20.	Bought goods on credit from J. T. Smith . . .	30·00
22.	Sold goods on credit to M. Crossley	50·00

Dr.			PURCHASES ACCOUNT			Cr.
19.. Jan. 20	J. T. Smith . .		£ 30			£

Dr.			J. T. SMITH			Cr.
		£	19.. Jan. 20	Purchases . .		£ 30

Dr.   SALES ACCOUNT   Cr.

| | | | £ | 19..
Jan. 22 | M. Crossley   . | | £
50 |

Dr.   M. CROSSLEY   Cr.

| 19..
Jan. 22 | Sales   .   .   . | | £
50 | | | | £ |

Note that the Purchases Account contains a record of all purchases of goods for resale whether for cash or on credit. Similarly, all sales for cash and on credit are entered in the Sales Account. J. T. Smith's Account above is credited because he parts with the goods, whilst £50 is placed on the debit of M. Crossley's account as he receives the goods sold to him.

If we pay J. T. Smith £30 on, say, 20th February, and M. Crossley pays us £50 on 22nd February, then the following entries are required—

Credit Cash Account £30 as it is paid out.

Debit J. T. Smith's Account as he receives it.

Credit M. Crossley's Account with £50 as he pays out that sum.

Debit Cash Account as we receive it.

The personal accounts of Smith and Crossley will then appear as below, showing nothing due to or owing by them—

Dr.   J. T. SMITH   Cr.

| 19..
Feb. 20 | Cash   .   .   . | | £
30 | 19..
Jan. 20 | Purchases   . | | £
30 |

Dr.   M. CROSSLEY   Cr.

| 19..
Jan. 22 | Sales   .   . | | £
50 | 19..
Feb. 22 | Cash   .   . | | £
50 |

These personal accounts of customers are essential as at any time we may require to know the amount due to or from a customer. They follow the principle of all Ledger accounts, that of grouping together under one heading similar or related items.

As a trader's transactions are mainly on credit and cash purchases and sales are less usual, the words "on credit" in exercises are often omitted. "Bought goods £50 from T. Jones" should be treated as a *credit* purchase—that is, all transactions should be dealt with as on credit unless otherwise mentioned.

Purchases

A trader buys goods for the purpose of selling them at a profit. As already explained, a record of these is kept in the Purchases Account and Sales Account. There are, however, other purchases in the ordinary course of business but not made with the intention of selling. The trader may buy an office desk, a typewriter, or a filing cabinet for his office, and, perhaps, a pair of scales for his shop. These are not bought for subsequent sale but to keep and use for as long as possible. Such purchases cannot be entered in the Purchases Account, reserved as it is for purchases for subsequent sale, but must be entered in accounts headed specially for them. For example, I buy an office desk for £10 in cash. I should *credit* Cash Account and *debit* an account headed "Furniture and Fittings" to which I put all such items of furniture and office equipment as are bought for more or less permanent use.

Dr.		FURNITURE AND FITTINGS			*Cr.*
19.. Jan. 10	Cash . . .	£ 10			£

Should I purchase the business premises and not rent them, I must keep an account for that purchase, as I certainly do not intend to sell them immediately for profit as in the case of goods in the shop. The Cash Account would be credited with the purchase price and a new account opened as below.

Dr.			PREMISES			Cr.
19.. Jan. 11	Cash . . .		£ 4,800			£

A third form of purchase is of such articles as string, postage stamps, office stationery, etc. These, however, are used up in the ordinary course of business and are an expense to the firm. They are bought neither to keep nor to sell again, and because they lessen the profit are debited to the Profit and Loss Account as expenses of running the business. The Cash Account is, of course, credited if they are bought for cash.

Credit transactions and the purchase of office furniture and similar goods to keep, will extend the list of assets and liabilities with which the student is at present acquainted. Debtors, that is, those owing the business something are included among the assets, whilst the creditors, those to whom the business owes something, are placed with the other liabilities. Property in any form bought to keep is an asset and should appear under that heading in the Balance Sheet.

EXERCISE 18

Record the following transactions in K. Thompson's Ledger on double-entry principles and take out a Trial Balance—

		£
Jan.	1. K. Thompson commenced business with capital in cash	400·00
	4. Bought goods for cash	300·00
	7. Sold goods on credit to W. White	160·00
	11. Sold goods on credit to B. Brown	86·00
	15. Sold goods for cash	100·00
	20. Paid transport expenses	5·00
	28. Paid wages	10·00
	Paid for packing material	3·00
	29. B. Brown paid his account in cash.	
	30. W. White paid on account	60·00

(Cash Balance, £328. Trial Balance totals, £746.)

Prepare final accounts as at 30th January. Stock on hand, £110.

(Gross Profit, £156. Net Profit, £138. Balance Sheet totals, £538.)

EXERCISE 19

Arthur White started business on 12th March, 19.., with capital in cash £150. Open his Ledger accounts and record the following transactions—

		£
Mar. 12.	Bought new shelves and racks for shop and paid cash .	20·00
14.	Bought quantity of tweeds and suitings from Yorkshire Woollens Co.	70·00
16.	Bought serges from Scottish Mills Co. . .	50·00
18.	Sold for cash, tweeds	36·00
24.	Sold to J. Durham, serge	25·00
25.	Paid railway charges	4·00
29.	Sold to J. Wilson, cloth	10·00
30.	Paid assistant, cash	10·00

Extract Trial Balance.

(Cash Balance, £152. Trial Balance totals, £341.)

Prepare final accounts as at 31st March. Stock on hand, £80.

(Gross Profit, £31. Net Profit, £17. Balance Sheet totals, £287.)

EXERCISE 20

J. Robinson commenced business as cycle dealer with £100 capital in cash on 9th June, 19... Open the necessary Ledger accounts to record this and the following transactions—

		£
June 10.	Bought fixtures (bench, etc.) for workshop (*debit* Fixtures Account)	21·00
12.	Bought six cycles at £5 each from J. Raylee & Co. .	30·00
14.	Bought six cycles at £4 each from Meed & Sons .	24·00
16.	Sold for cash two cycles at £8·40 each .	16·80
18.	Sold to J. Leonard & Co. six cycles at £6·30 each	37·80
24.	Bought four second-hand cycles for cash . .	4·50
26.	Sundry cash sales	1·68
28.	Paid J. Raylee & Co.	30·00
30.	Paid sundry expenses	2·00

Take out Trial Balance.

(Cash Balance, £60·98. Trial Balance totals, £180·28.)

Prepare final accounts. Stock on hand at 30th June, £24.

(Gross Profit, £21·78. Net Profit, £19·78. Balance Sheet totals, £143·78.)

EXERCISE 21

S. Carter commenced business on 1st January with capital in cash £120. Open the necessary accounts to record the above and the following transactions—

			£
Jan.	1.	Bought goods for cash	20·00
	2.	Bought goods from Weston & Sons . . .	85·50
	4.	Bought scales for shop and paid cash . .	15·00
	7.	Cash sales	36·00
	9.	Bought two delivery cycles on credit from the London	
		Cycle Co.	32·00
	17.	Cash sales to date	40·00
	18.	Paid boy's wages	3·80
	24.	Paid Weston & Sons	85·50
	25.	Bought more goods from Weston & Sons . .	56·00
		Paid boy's wages	3·80
	31.	Cash sales to date	38·75

Take out Trial Balance.

(Cash Balance, £106·65.   Trial Balance totals, £322·75.)

Prepare final accounts as at 31st January.   Stock on hand, £106.

(Gross Profit, £59·25.   Net Profit, £51·65.   Balance Sheet totals, £259·65.)

ADDITIONAL EXERCISES

Graded Book-keeping Exercises, Nos. 11 to 19.

CHAPTER VII

BANKS AND BANKING

THE greater part of retail trading is conducted on a *cash* basis. Most shopkeepers expect their customers to pay cash for the goods they purchase. The housewife pays cash for the food she buys for her family and the student will probably pay cash for his or her books and stationery. However, most business transactions (apart from retail sales) are completed on the basis of *credit*. Illustrations of credit transactions are given in Chapter VI and show clearly that goods are supplied many days or even weeks before payment is made. Moreover, suppliers such as manufacturers and importers seldom supply goods only to businesses situated nearby. Most suppliers have customers (merchants, dealers, wholesalers and retailers) in many parts of the country. Payment for goods supplied must therefore be made through the post and, since it is both inconvenient and risky to send cash (notes and coins) through the post, settlement of business debts is usually made by cheque. The use of cheques for payments of sums of money is confined to those who have bank accounts and it is therefore appropriate at this stage to describe some of the work of the banks and, in particular, how they operate the cheque system.

The main function of a commercial bank is to receive money deposited by its customers and to pay out money in accordance with the orders given by those customers. These orders are generally in the form of *cheques*. The bank must, of course, keep account of money deposited and amounts paid out and will usually make a charge for its services. Some customers of the bank may wish to borrow money and, subject to agreement, a customer is allowed to *overdraw* his account. A bank customer's account is said to be *overdrawn* when cheques have been

34

issued to a total value greater than the total amount of money deposited. Interest is charged by the bank on the amount overdrawn. Thus banks obtain much of their income by making a charge for their services and by charging interest on the money borrowed by customers.

The most significant part of the work of a commercial bank is the operation of the cheque system. A cheque is a written order drawn up and signed by the customer of the bank (known as the *drawer*) on which he instructs the bank to pay a certain sum of money to a specified person or firm. Cheques are normally made out on the printed cheque forms provided by the bank. An illustration of a completed cheque is shown on the next page.

In this case the *drawer* of the cheque, J. Jones, is a customer of Barclays Bank Ltd., High Street, Anytown, and he is instructing the bank to pay £4·27 to J. Browne. The cheque is dated at the top right-hand side and in the space provided, between the words "Pay" and "or Order", J. Jones has entered the name of the person (or firm) to whom the sum is to be paid. In this case J. Browne is the *payee* (the one to be paid). On the lines underneath, the amount to be paid is shown in *words* and in the box provided this sum is stated again in *figures*. The cheque is signed at the bottom right-hand side on the line underneath the box. Many banks *personalize* their cheques by printing the name of the account holder immediately beneath the box, although there is no legal requirement for this.

The law on this subject is complex and much of it need not concern us here. However, students should know that the Bills of Exchange Act, 1882, defines a cheque (in Section 73) as—

A Bill of Exchange, drawn on a banker, payable on demand.

Up-to-date rules governing cheques are contained in the Cheques Act, 1957.

The illustration of the cheque shown on page 36 contains four groups of numbers. The first of these is at the top right-hand corner, next to the date. The number 20–63–19 is the code number of the Barclays Bank, High Street, Anytown.

15 Feb 1973   20-63-19

BARCLAYS BANK LIMITED

HIGH STREET, ANYTOWN

Pay J. Browne _____ or Order

Four Pounds and

Twenty seven pence only

£ 4 - 27

J. Jones

⑆049624⑆ 20⑉6319⑉ 42 808 6⑈

All Barclays Bank branches have code numbers starting with the figure 2; all Midland branches begin with the figure 4; Lloyds branches 3; and so on. This number is repeated in magnetized computer printing (which can be "read" by automatic data processing equipment) at the base of the cheque. In the same sort of printing are two other groups of figures. On the left is the serial number of the cheque; on the right is the account number of the *drawer*, J. Jones.

Some explanation is needed of the words "or Order" which are printed after the space for the payee's name. Readers may have seen cheques with the words "or Bearer" printed in this position. These words indicate the procedure necessary when a cheque is cashed or passed on to another person. An "order" cheque must be *endorsed* when it is cashed or passed on. The *payee* endorses a cheque by signing it on the reverse, using exactly the same name and initials as shown on the face. J. Browne should endorse the cheque by signing on the reverse "J. Browne." An authorized representative could sign on his behalf, e.g. "for J. Browne, F. White, Secretary"; "J. A. Browne" would be an irregular endorsement. "Bearer" cheques require no endorsement and can be cashed at the counter of the bank on which they are drawn by the *payee* or any "bearer."

The cheque illustrated on page 36 is a *crossed* cheque. That is to say it has two parallel lines printed vertically across the face. The words "& Co" may or may not be printed between these two lines. These words have no legal effect and are written or printed inside the crossing as a matter of convention. The effect of crossing a cheque is that it cannot be cashed at the bank on which it is drawn and must be paid in to the credit of a bank account. The lines are, in fact, an instruction to the paying banker to pay only to another banker and are said to constitute a *general crossing*. Clearly, cheques sent through the post should be crossed to minimize the risk of theft. A person who pays a cheque in to the credit of his account can be traced, so a crossed cheque is of little use to a thief. A further safeguard is obtained by writing the words "not negotiable" between the parallel lines. This does not, in fact, prevent

negotiation (passing of the cheque from one person to another).
Therefore, if the *payee* of a cheque has no bank account, he can
exchange it for cash with someone who has an account, even
though the words "not negotiable" appear on the crossing.
The effect of a "not negotiable" crossing is to prevent any
holder of the cheque gaining a better right to it than the
previous holder. Thus a thief could not settle one of his own
debts by passing on a cheque crossed "not negotiable."
However, anyone who agrees to accept a stolen cheque with a
general crossing and without the words *not negotiable* on the
crossing may well obtain a good right to the money so long as
he does not *know* it was stolen. By far the best safeguard
against loss by fraud or theft is obtained by giving a cheque
a *special crossing*.

If the *drawer* knows the name of the *payee*'s bank and writes
the name and address of the bank between the lines, the
cheque can then only be paid through that bank. The addition
of the words "account payee only" effectively prevents the
cheque being placed to the credit of any account but that of the
dayee.

Before agreeing to open an account for a potential customer
a banker will usually require the applicant to provide the names
of persons from whom references as to character and respect-
ability can be obtained. The type of account into which money
is paid and against which cheques are drawn is known as a
Current Account. A large and growing number of private
individuals as well as businesses hold Current Accounts. In
some cases, mainly when the customer guarantees to maintain
a stated minimum balance in the account, the banker may
agree to make no charge for keeping the account. It is likely
to be of interest to many readers that many British banks
make no charge for keeping a student's Current Account
providing the student does not overdraw or require any special
services. However, most Current Accounts are debited in
respect of *changes* on 1st January and 1st July each year. The
amount charged will depend on the amount of work involved
in keeping the account.

Another type of account is the Deposit Account. If there is a large balance on Current Account not likely to be required immediately, the customer may request the bank to transfer a certain sum to a Deposit Account. Money placed to Deposit Account cannot be drawn upon by cheque, and banks require, under ordinary circumstances, at least seven days' notice of the wish to withdraw sums from deposit. Interest is allowed on such sums as the bank knows it has the use of the money for a definite period. Should the money be required the bank may be asked to transfer the whole or part back again to Current Account when it is again available to be drawn on by cheque.

Banks provide their customers with a copy of their accounts either at fixed intervals (often monthly) or when a Ledger sheet has been filled with entries. Copies of customers' Ledger accounts are known as *Bank Statements* and are also available to customers on request or at short notice. Statements are usually sent to customers through the post but they can be handed over at the bank if this is required. Most banks provide a plastic folder so that customers can file their statements neatly.

When making payments into the bank, paying-in slips are filled up on which is stated the amount to be paid in and the form it takes, whether cash, notes, or cheques. A duplicate copy is initialled by the bank cashier and handed back to the customer as an acknowledgement of the money paid in.

CHAPTER VIII

THE BANK ACCOUNT AND ITS OPERATION

THE exercises in earlier chapters have involved payments in cash only. We have now to consider the entries required when cheques also are used as means of payment. In practice little cash is kept in the office, and much use is made of the Bank Account. There is less likelihood of loss by fire or theft, and, as already pointed out, cheques are the cheapest and safest means of making payments.

The example given below is a simplified series of transactions involving cash and cheques.

			£
Jan.	1.	Cash in hand, £42. Cash at bank, £120.	
	2.	Paid M. Smith by cheque	21·50
	3.	Paid Transport Account in cash	1·30
	4.	Received cheque from L. Smart	31·00
	5.	Paid M. James by cheque	40·00
	9.	Cash sales to date	18·00
	10.	E. Unwin paid his account by cheque . . .	60·00
	15.	Bought goods and paid by cheque . . .	76·00
	22.	Cash sales to date	10·80
	26.	Paid cash for postage stamps	2·00
	31.	Paid wages in cash	18·00

The working of this example is shown below, though the double-entry is ignored for the purpose of this chapter. The Cash Account follows the ordinary type with which we are now familiar, but the cheques received and cheques paid away have been recorded in a Bank Account.

Dr.				CASH ACCOUNT				Cr.
19. .				£	19. .			£
Jan. 1	Balance . .	b/d	42·00	Jan. 3	Transport Expenses . .		1·30
9	Cash Sales . .		18·00	26	Postage Stamps . .		2·00
22	Cash Sales . .		10·80	31	Wages . .		18·00
					Balance . .	c/d	49·50
			£70·80				£70·80
Feb. 1	Balance . .	b/d	49·50				

Dr.					BANK ACCOUNT				Cr.
19..				£	19..				£
Jan. 1	Balance	.	b/d	120·00	Jan. 2	M. Smith .	.		21·50
4	L. Smart	.		31·00	5	M. James .	.		40·00
10	E. Unwin	.		60·00	15	Cash			
						Purchases	.		76·00
					31	Balance .	.	c/d	73·50
				£211·00					£211·00
Feb. 1	Balance	.	b/d	73·50					

Both these accounts are Ledger accounts. The Bank
Account is a record of payments into the bank and withdrawals
from the bank. The former appear on the debit side, the
latter on the credit side. It is common practice to pay into the
bank all cheques the day they are received. An item that
mentions a cheque being received from a customer should be
debited to the Bank Account as if the cheque was paid at once
into the bank. Payments by cheque are entered at once to the
credit of the Bank Account, as the bank parts with the money
on cheques being presented for payment. The balance of this
account shows, of course, the amount that should be in the
possession of the bank at the time of balancing.

Trace carefully the items in the given example until they are
discovered in the two accounts.

The Two-column Cash Book

Though the Cash and Bank Accounts are Ledger accounts,
they are usually kept in a book separate from the general
Ledger. This is purely a matter of convenience, as it enables
the cashier to keep the accounts entered up to date without
interfering with the use of the Ledger for other purposes.
This separation does not alter the fact that they are still
Ledger accounts and form an integral part of double-entry
book-keeping. A further convenience, that enables the cash
and bank balances to be ascertained at a glance without
turning to separate accounts, is the form of ruling known as a
double- (or two-) column Cash Book. The two accounts
shown previously have been combined in the example (a)
shown on p. 43 to form a double-column Cash Book.

It will be seen that this Cash Book takes its name from there being two £ columns on each side. The double-column account is formed by taking the debit column of the Bank Account and placing it alongside the debit column of the Cash Account, and, similarly, with the credit sides of the two accounts. Bearing this in mind, the preparation of a two-column Cash Account should present no difficulties.

The following items are selected from the example given on p. 40.

							£
1.	Jan.	2.	Paid M. Smith by cheque	.	.	.	21·50
2.		3.	Paid Transport Account in cash	.	.	.	1·30
3.		4.	Received cheque from L. Smart	.	.	.	31·00
4.		22.	Cash sales .	.	.	.	10·80

Take each item separately and notice where it appears in the separate Cash or Bank Account on pp. 40–41. Now find the item in the worked example of the double-column Cash Book, and the simplicity of the latter is apparent. The two cash columns and the two bank columns in the combined account are balanced separately and the balances carried down to the appropriate columns for the next period.

Payments from Cash into Bank

When too much cash for immediate needs is in the office the whole or part of it is paid into the bank. In the above examples the double-entry aspect of the transactions has been ignored in order to simplify the explanation, but in considering such an item as—

Jan. 6. Paid £50 from Office Cash into Bank

the double-entry cannot be ignored as it affects both the Cash and Bank Accounts. Cash is paid out to the extent of £50 and the bank receives that sum. To record the first aspect, £50 must be credited to the Cash Account. To record the other aspect, £50 must be debited to the Bank Account. The double-entry for this transaction is therefore contained in the two accounts, viz., Cash Account and Bank Account. This is just as true when these two accounts are combined in the double-column Cash Book.

(a)

DOUBLE-COLUMN CASH BOOK

Dr. / Cr.

Date	Particulars	Fol.	Cash £	Bank £	Date	Particulars	Fol.	Cash £	Bank £
19.. Jan. 1	Balance	b/d	42·00	120·00	19.. Jan. 2	M. Smith			21·50
4	L. Smart			31·00	3	Transport Expenses		1·30	
9	Cash Sales		18·00		5	M. James			40·00
10	E. Unwin			60·00	15	Cash Purchases			76·00
22	Cash Sales		10·80		26	Postage Stamps		2·00	
					31	Wages		18·00	
						Balance	c/d	49·50	73·50
			£70·80	£211·00				£70·80	£211·00
Feb. 1	Balance	b/d	49·50	73·50					

(b)

CASH BOOK

Dr. / Cr.

Date	Particulars	Fol.	Cash £	Bank £	Date	Particulars	Fol.	Cash £	Bank £
19.. Jan. 6	Cash	c.		50·00	19.. Jan. 6	Bank	c.		20·00
10	Bank	c.	20·00		10	Cash	c.	50·00	

Withdrawals from Bank for Office Cash

At other times there may not be sufficient cash in the office to meet the payments required to be made in cash in the near future. The cashier on such occasions cashes a cheque and the action he takes would be worded in an exercise somewhat as follows—

Jan. 10. Drew from the bank for Office Cash, £20

The bank pays out and the office cash receives £20. The entries required are: debit Cash Account with the £20 received and credit Bank Account with the £20 paid out.

In the double-column Cash Book the £20 would appear on the credit side in the column headed "Bank" and on the debit side in the column headed "Cash."

These two items, cash from bank and cash paid into bank, would appear in the double-column Cash Book as shown at (*b*) on p. 43.

Bank Overdraft and Loans

In Chapter VII it was noted that an important function of a bank is to lend money to its customers. The usual procedure is for the customer to approach his banker for permission to *overdraw* his account and, subject to certain conditions, the banker will usually agree. After all, bankers make more revenue from interest and charges than they would be able to earn from charges alone. A banker always asks three important questions of a customer who applies for an *overdraft* or *loan*. These are—

1. How much?
2. For how long?
3. What security can you offer, or what guarantee can you offer as to repayment?

Providing satisfactory answers are given to these questions and so long as the banker has funds available he will agree. Thus a customer may receive permission to overdraw his account to a maximum of, say, £500 on the understanding that the advance will be repaid before a stated date.

When an *overdraft* facility is granted no special entries are made in the books. The customer issues cheques to the full amount already deposited and can continue to issue cheques thereafter until the limit of £500 is reached. Of course, when he pays in sums of money, whether in cash or cheques, the *overdraft* is reduced by the amount of such credits. The Cash Book of a bank customer who has overdrawn his account might show entries as follows—

Dr.					CASH BOOK (Bank columns only)			*Cr.*
			Bank					Bank
19.. June 30	Previous Items amount to		£	19.. June 30	Previous Items amount to			£
	Balance .	. c/d	1,736 70		T. Smith .	.		1,656 150
			£1,806					£1,806
				July 1	Balance .	. b/d		70

Before paying Smith, on 30th June there was a balance of £80 in the bank. After paying £150 the account is £70 *overdrawn*. An overdrawn bank balance is brought down on the *credit* side, since the bank is a *creditor* for the amount overdrawn. If this account holder were later to pay £30 into the bank this would reduce the adverse balance to £40. The bank column of the Cash Book would be debited £30, thus bringing the credit (adverse) balance on the bank column down from £70 to £40.

Interest is charged on *overdrafts* at the end of each half year, 30th June and 31st December, but the bank charges interest only on the amount by which the account is actually overdrawn. Thus, if the account illustrated is left at £70 overdrawn for one month and is then increased to £170 overdrawn, the bank will charge *one* month's interest (1/12 of the annual rate) on £70 and *five* months' interest (5/12 of the annual rate) on £170 when the accounts are balanced on 31st December.

If a bank customer requires a loan for a relatively long period and an overdraft does not seem appropriate, the bank may make a loan of a fixed sum—say £1,000. In such a case the customer's account at the bank is credited £1,000 and the bank's customer should *debit* the bank column of his Cash Book £1,000 and *credit* this sum to a Bank Loan Account. Interest is charged on the *full amount* of the loan until it is repaid.

It should be noted that the customer's account in the *bank's books* is the reverse of the customer's entries in the bank column of his own Cash Book. A *debit* in the bank column of the Cash Book appears as a *credit* in the customer's account in the bank's books. When the customer issues a cheque he *credits* the bank column of his Cash Book and when this cheque is received by the bank for payment the banker will *debit* the customer's account.

A Bank Loan Account or overdraft should appear as a *liability* in the Balance Sheet since it represents money owed by the business. Interest payments, whether for loan or overdraft, are *credited* in the bank column of the Cash Book and debited to Interest Account. At the end of the business's financial year, Interest Account is credited and the Profit and Loss Account debited with the total amount of interest paid. Thus interest is shown as a cost of running the business.

Deposit Accounts

Should the bank be requested to transfer an amount from Current Account to Deposit Account (as mentioned in the preceding chapter), the Bank Account in the Cash Book is credited by that sum and the debit entry is made in an account in the Ledger headed "Bank Deposit Account." On sums being returned by the bank from Deposit Account to Current Account it will be necessary to debit the Bank Account in the Cash Book and credit the Deposit Account in the Ledger. The balance remaining on Deposit Account when the Balance Sheet is prepared must be shown among the assets along with the balance on Current Account.

Interest given by the bank is debited to the Bank Account

in the Cash Book and credited to an *Interest Received Account*. At the end of the trading period the balance of the Interest Received Account is transferred to Profit and Loss Account and represents a gain.

EXERCISE 22

Write up the following transactions in the Cash Book (with Cash and Bank columns), ignoring the double-entry for this exercise. Cheques are paid into bank daily—

		£
Jan.	1. Cash in hand	23·50
	Cash at bank	114·57
	3. Paid L. James by cheque	18·37
	4. Paid travelling expenses in cash	3·50
	6. Received cheque from P. Newman . . .	18·33
	9. Paid B. Matthews by cheque	14·70
	10. Cash sales to date	27·57
	13. Paid advertisement charges in cash . . .	8·50
	16. Bought typewriter sundries for cash . . .	0·52
	20. Received cash from L. Kemp	1·20
	24. J. Fyson paid his account by cheque . . .	23·80
	30. Cash sales	10·11
	31. Paid J. Thompson & Sons by cheque . . .	2·52

Balance the accounts as at 31st January.

(Cash Balance, £49·86. Bank Balance, £121·11.

EXERCISE 23

Treat as preceding Exercise 22.

		£
July	1. F. Brighton commenced business with cash in bank	800·00
	2. Cashed cheque for office cash	40·00
	3. Paid sundry expenses in cash	3·17
	4. Bought goods and paid by cheque . . .	140·61
	8. Cash sales to date	86·50
	9. Paid cash into bank	80·00
	12. Received cheque from P. Lewes . . .	26·00
	17. Bought goods for cash	18·90
	19. Cash sales to date	78·92
	Paid cash into bank	75·00
	24. Paid M. Newhaven by cheque	211·21
	27. Paid cash for stationery	1·50
	31. Drew from bank for office cash	15·00

Balance the accounts as at 31st July.

(Cash balance, £41·85. Bank Balance, £574·18.)

EXERCISE 24

Record the following transactions in the necessary Ledger accounts and two-column Cash Book. Take out Trial Balance as at 30th April—

		£
Apr. 1. M. Cox started business with—		
Cash at bank		640·00
Cash in hand		73·50
2. Bought goods from T. Larcombe		124·80
3. Bought goods from F. Gloster		42·00
6. Sold goods to D. Daniels & Sons		187·25
8. Bought office desk for cash		10·50
12. Paid cash for stationery		2·60
14. Paid F. Gloster his account by cheque		42·00
16. Sold goods for cash		28·00
17. Drew cheque for self		10·00
20. D. Daniels paid their account as to £180 by cheque and remainder in cash.		
28. Paid one month's rent by cheque		12·00
29. Cash sales		17·05
30. Paid cash into bank		80·00

(Cash Balance, £32·70. Bank Balance, £836. Trial Balance totals, £1070·60.)
Prepare final accounts as at 30th April. Stock on hand £33.
(Gross Profit, £98·50. Net Profit, £83·90. Balance Sheet totals, £912·20.)

EXERCISE 25

Enter the following transactions in F. Newton's Ledger and Cash Book (Cash and Bank columns)—

		£
July 1. F. Newton commenced business with—		
Cash at bank		940·00
Cash in hand		66·50
2. Bought from J. Thomas, goods		210·00
3. Placed on Deposit Account at bank		500·00
5. Bought for cash, goods		20·50
8. Sold to R. Macdonald, goods		170·00
12. Cash purchases		30·00
15. Drew from bank for office cash		50·00
17. Paid J. Thomas by cheque		210·00
18. Paid travellers' expenses in cash		27·50
21. Cash sales		60·00
25. Bought and paid by cheque goods		150·00
27. Withdrew from Deposit to Current Account		300·00

Take out Trial Balance as at 31st July.
(Cash Balance, £98·50. Bank Balances: Current Account, £330. Deposit Account, £200. Trial Balance totals, £1,236·50.)
Prepare final accounts as at 31st July. Stock on hand at that date, £255.
(Gross Profit, £74·50. Net Profit, £47·00. Balance Sheet totals, £1,053·50.)

ADDITIONAL EXERCISES
Graded Book-keeping Exercises, Nos. 20 to 31.

CHAPTER IX

THE JOURNAL

It was stated in the first chapter that, in its simplest form, double-entry book-keeping requires two books for its operation, namely, the Journal and the Ledger. The latter, as the more important, has already been explained: it is now appropriate to consider the Journal.

The word "journal" as shown by dictionary definition can mean "a book containing private record of events as they occur day by day." The functions of the Journal in book-keeping can be described as (*a*) acting as a diary in which events (business transactions) are recorded as they occur; (*b*) acting as a *book of explanation*, since after each entry is recorded a brief explanatory note called a *narration*; and (*c*) acting as a *book of instruction*, since it states which accounts in the Ledger are to be debited and which to be credited.

A simple rule to remember is: *The Journal tells you what to put in the Ledger: it tells you which account to debit and which to credit.*

Originally, all entries were first made in the Journal and then entered in the Ledger, but this proved to be wasteful for ordinary sales and purchases of goods for which no explanations or *narrations* were necessary. Routine payments and receipts of cash similarly required no explanation so such entries are now posted straight to the Ledger. In some small businesses credit sales and purchases may still be entered in a *General Journal* but, more generally, a special *Bought Journal* and *Sales Journal* are used.

Briefly, the situation can be summed up thus—

All Credit Entries (those in which no cash changed hands)— into the Journal first.

Unusual Cash Entries—All such cash transactions as the purchase or sale of assets (cash here includes bank entries)—into the Journal first.

Ordinary Cash Entries (ordinary receipts and payments requiring no explanation)—straight into the Ledger.

Another simple rule to remember is: *Transactions, except for routine cash entries and sales and purchases of goods, are entered first in the Journal.*

Thus an item "Paid Rates in cash (or by cheque)" would be entered straight into the Ledger, because although rates may be paid quarterly or half-yearly, they are an ordinary, common expense needing no explanation.

On the other hand a business will buy, say, a typewriter only very occasionally and this will need recording in the Journal whether bought on credit or for cash. The entry would appear as follows—

JOURNAL

19..			£	£
Jan. 5	Office Equipment Account . . .	L.17	65	
	Bank Account	CB.1		65
	Purchase of "Rite-well" typewriter serial no. 784326 for use in Sales Office. .			

Note that entries to be debited in the Ledger always appear first, followed by the entries to be credited, and then the "narration" is given.

Note also that in the folio column "L.17" appears against the item to be debited. This indicates that on p. 17 of the Ledger a debit has been placed to Office Equipment Account. The entry "CB.1" against the item to be credited indicates that on p. 1 of the Cash Book a credit entry in respect of the purchase of and payment for a typewriter has been made.

Opening Journal Entries

In the first place the capital of a business usually consists of cash. But in setting up the business this original cash capital must be expended on various forms of property, e.g. a stock of goods for sale, fittings and fixtures, and delivery vans or cycles, and, perhaps, premises. Hitherto we have been concerned only with the simple accounts of traders who had little need for assets other than cash in hand or at bank. But as the business grows the need for an adequate record of transactions and of property held becomes more and more imperative. On deciding to keep his books on double-entry principles or on opening a new set of books, the trader summarizes his financial position. This summary will disclose that he has certain assets, valuable possessions, as mentioned above. In addition certain sums of money may be owing to him by customers, whilst, on the other hand, he may owe various sums. The latter are his liabilities, and, taking the total of these from his assets, he is able to say what he is worth financially. That amount by which his assets exceed his liabilities is called his capital. This summary is made in the Journal and is one of the special uses to which the Journal is put. Many book-keeping exercises commence by requiring such a summary to be made, but in practice it will seldom happen more than once in the lifetime of a business.

Example

B. Bath decides to open a set of books on double-entry principles. His business affairs on 1st July, 19.., stand as follows: Office cash, £33; bank balance, £282; value of premises, £1,200; stock of goods, £420; two debtors, B. Green and L. Brown owe him £72 and £30 respectively. He owes two creditors, W. Atkins and A. Elmitt, £40 and £38, respectively.

The opening entries in his Journal would be as follows—

JOURNAL

19..								£	£
July 1	Office Cash .	.	.	.	.	.	CB	33	
	Cash at Bank	.	.	.	.	.	CB	282	
	Premises	.	.	.	.	.	L.1	1,200	
	Stock .	.	.	.	.	.	L.2	420	
	B. Green	.	.	.	.	.	L.3	72	
	L. Brown	.	.	.	.	.	L.4	30	
	W. Atkins.	.	.	.	.	.	L.5		40
	A. Elmitt .	.	.	.	.	.	L.6		38
	Capital	.	.	.	.	.	L.7		1,959
	Assets, liabilities, and capital at this date .	.	.	.	.	.		£2,037	£2,037

The items in the above opening entries are then posted to the Ledger, the assets being *debited* to the respective Asset Accounts, the cash and bank balances in the Cash Book, the stock to the Stock Account, the value of the premises to the Premises Account, and the debts due to the respective debtors' accounts. The liabilities are posted to the credit of the respective accounts and the capital to the credit of the Capital Account, as showing the amount left in the business by the owner and the extent which it is indebted to him. The appropriate folio numbers are, of course, inserted.

The entries in the Ledger accounts are usually described in the particulars column as "Balance" as they usually represent the balances of accounts brought down from the previous period. Opening entries, as shown in the example, will usually be entered as "Sundries" in the Ledger.

These items having been posted, the books are ready for the transactions to be entered as and when they occur. In working exercises and in examination tests it is especially necessary to post the opening entries before commencing to enter the transactions, as otherwise sums due or owing may be overlooked.

If, by way of illustrating the use of the Journal, the opening entries and *all* the transactions in Exercise 30 at the end of the next chapter were to be *journalized*, i.e., entered in the Journal, the result would be as shown below—

JOURNAL—L. AMERY

19.. Jan. 1		£	£
	Cash	63·50	
	Bank	240·00	
	Stock	360·00	
	Capital		663·50
	Assets representing capital at this date.		
		£663·50	£663·50

JOURNAL—L. AMERY—(*Continued*)

			£	£
Jan. 5	Purchases Account		175·00	
	T. Griffiths			175·00
	Goods bought for resale. (*Give details.*)			
7	Shop Fittings Account		24·50	
	Bank Account			24·50
	Fittings (*give details*) bought for use in shop.			
12	G. Soames		85·00	
	Sales Account			85·00
	Goods sold on credit.			
23	Purchases Account		64·00	
	F. Barton			64·00
	Goods bought on credit.			
27	M. Cranford		130·00	
	Sales Account			130·00
	Goods sold on credit.			
28	Shop Fittings Account		40·00	
	Bank Account			40·00
	Cash register bought for use in shop.			

The fact that no folio numbers are shown indicates that none of these entries has been made in the Ledger as yet.

EXERCISE 26

From the following particulars prepare the Journal entry in order to open the books of G. Harrison as on 1st January, 19.., showing his capital—

		£
Cash in hand		27·50
Cash at bank		143·00
Stock		350·00
Debtors: N. Crocker		24·10
C. Bradshaw		49·50
Creditors: G. Nunn		23·40
W. Egerton		52·50

EXERCISE 27

Prepare the necessary Journal entry to open D. Westley's books on 1st July 19.., his assets and liabilities being as follows—

		£
Cash in hand	. . . . . .	31·00
Cash at bank	. . . . . .	200·00
Stock	. . . . . .	400·00
Office furniture	. . . . . .	70·00
Premises	. . . . . .	1,000·00
Motor vans	. . . . . .	350·00
Debtors: R. Tilt	. . . . . .	67·00
E. Crocker	. . . . .	39·00
Creditor: L. Bridges	. . . . .	40·00

EXERCISE 28

Ascertain R. Courtney's capital as on 1st January and prepare the Journal entry necessary to open the books on that date. His financial position was as follows—

		£
Cash in hand	. . . . . .	29·00
Stock	. . . . . .	320·00
Debtors: R. Smith	. . . . .	60·00
B. Jones	. . . . .	30·00
Creditor: L. Southerst	. . . .	56·00
Premises	. . . . . .	900·00
Bank overdraft	. . . . . .	184·00

EXERCISE 29

R. Watson's affairs stood as follows on 1st January. Prepare the Journal entry necessary to open his books—

		£
Cash at bank	. . . . . .	500·00
Cash in hand	. . . . . .	25·40
Furniture and fittings	. . . .	210·00
Stock	. . . . . .	424·00
Debtors: R. Green	. . . . .	180·00
J. Brown	. . . . .	240·00
Creditor: R. Read	. . . . .	194·50

ADDITIONAL EXERCISES
Graded Book-keeping Exercises, Nos. 32 to 35.

CHAPTER X

THE STOCK ACCOUNT

THE item of stock at start, representing the value of goods on hand at the beginning of a trading period, requires further explanation. The stock at close of a trading period has been discussed in Chapter IV. The stock at close becomes the stock on hand with which the *new* period is commenced, and it is more than probable that it will be disposed of, along with current purchases, during the next period of trading. It must therefore be taken into account in ascertaining the gross profit.

The item "Stock £420" appearing in the Opening Entries on p. 51 in the preceding chapter will be posted to the Stock Account in the Ledger as follows—

Dr.				STOCK ACCOUNT				Cr.
19.. Jul. 1	Balance .	.	J	£ 420				£

Now let us assume that the purchases during the ensuing six months amounted to £800, sales to £1,300, and that stock-taking revealed £380 stock on hand on 31st December.

The stock on hand must be added to the purchases to obtain the total value of goods available for sale. But not all were sold, as the final stock-taking showed. The cost price of the goods that were sold may be ascertained thus—

						£
Stock at start	.	.	.	.	.	420
Add Purchases .	.	.	.	.	.	800
Total .	.	.	.	.	.	1,220
Less Stock remaining on hand	.	.	.	380
Cost price of goods sold .	.	.	.	£840

55

This figure (£840) deducted from the total sales (£1,300) yields the gross profit, viz., £460.

The book-keeping method is to transfer the stock *at start* from the Stock Account (thereby closing the latter) to the Trading Account. The purchases and sales are transferred from their respective accounts in the usual manner, and the entries for the stock *at close* are made by debiting the Stock Account for the new period with the value and crediting the Trading Account with a like sum.

The Stock Account and the Trading Account will then appear as follows—

Dr.   STOCK ACCOUNT   *Cr.*

19.. July 1	Balance	.	J	£ 420	19.. Dec. 31	Transfer to Trading A/c.	.		£ 420
19.. Jan. 1	Trading A/c.	.		380					

TRADING ACCOUNT

Dr.   FOR SIX MONTHS TO 31ST DECEMBER, 19..   *Cr.*

			£			£
Stock at Start	.		420	Sales . . .		1,300
Purchases	.		800	Stock at Close		380
Gross Profit .	. c/d		460			
			£1,680			£1,680

An alternative way of presenting the Trading Account, which is often used at present, is as follows—

TRADING ACCOUNT

Dr.   FOR SIX MONTHS TO 31ST DECEMBER, 19..   *Cr.*

			£			£
	Stock at start	.	420	Sales . . .		1,300
	Purchases	.	800			
			1,220			
Less	Stock at close	.	380			
	Cost of goods sold	.	840			
	Gross Profit	. c/d	460			
			1,300			1,300

EXERCISE 30

L. Amery's financial position on 1st January was as follows—

						£
Cash in hand	.	.	.	.	.	63·50
Cash at bank	.	.	.	.	.	240·00
Stock .	.	.	.	.	.	360·00

Open L. Amery's books by means of the Journal and enter the following transactions—

			£
Jan.	2.	Purchased for cash, goods	40·00
	5.	Bought from T. Griffiths, goods	175·00
	7.	Bought shop fittings and paid by cheque . .	24·50
	11.	Sales for cash	28·90
	12.	Sold to G. Soames, goods	85·00
	15.	Paid T. Griffiths by cheque on account . .	100·00
	18.	Cash sales	47·50
	19.	Paid cash into bank	80·00
	20.	Paid railway carriage cash	2·25
	23.	Bought goods from F. Barton . . .	64·00
	27.	Sold goods to M. Cranford . . .	130·00
	28.	Bought new cash register and paid by cheque . .	40·00
	31.	Paid rent of premises by cheque	15·00

Take out Trial Balance as at 31st January.

(Cash Balance £17·65. Bank Balance, £140·50. Trial Balance totals, £1,093·90.)

Prepare final accounts. Stock at 31st January, £420.

(Gross Profit, £72·40. Net Profit, £55·15. Balance Sheet totals, £857·65.)

EXERCISE 31

Treat as Exercise 30.

19..

Mar. 5. Cash in office, £10.
Balance in bank, £140.
Value of stock, £200.
Value of business premises, £1,750.

6. Sold to Frank Brown, 4 Bread Street, Southport—
12 reams foolscap paper at £0·35 a ream.
24 reams quarto paper at £0·20 a ream.

8. Bought 100 reams foolscap paper at 10p a ream and paid for it by cheque.

10. Sold for cash during the week—
20 reams foolscap paper at 25p a ream.
25 reams foolscap paper at 15p a ream
48 reams quarto paper at 12p a ream
Frank Brown paid his account in full in cash—
Paid into the bank, £20.
Paid trade expenses in cash, £4.
Balance of stock left, £196.

(Gross Profit, £9·51. Net Profit, £5·51. Balance Sheet totals, £2,105·51.)

(*U.L. & C.I.*)

EXERCISE 32

The affairs of D. Williamson at this date stood as follows—

	£
Cash in hand .	47·00
Cash at bank .	320·00
Stock in hand	560·00
Shop fittings .	100·00
Debtors: H. Crawley	70·00
W. Walton	36·00
Creditor: Gramophone Supply Co. .	120·00

Open D. Williamson's books and enter the following transactions—

	£
Dec. 2. Bought additional shop fittings for cash	20·00
7. Paid Gramophone Supply Co. by cheque .	120·00
10. Bought 20 gramophones and paid by cheque	105·00
12. Received cheque and paid into bank for gramophones sold	72·00
15. Bought from Gramophone Supply Co. 25 gramophones at £9 each	225·00
19. Sold to Johnson & Sons 10 gramophones at £17 each .	170·00
23. H. Crawley paid his account by cheque	70·00
27. Paid salaries by cheque	40·00
28. Cash sales to date .	66·00

Take out Trial Balance.

(Cash Balance, £93. Bank Balance, £197. Trial Balance totals, £1,546.)

Prepare final accounts. Stock in hand, 31st December, £670.

(Gross Profit, £88. Net Profit, £48. Balance Sheet totals, £1,286.)

ADDITIONAL EXERCISES

Graded Book-keeping Exercises, Nos. 36 and 43.

CHAPTER XI

THE BOUGHT JOURNAL AND BOUGHT LEDGER

So far, the student has learned the use of the Journal and the two volumes of the Ledger: (i) the Cash Book, containing two accounts, Cash and Bank, and (ii) the Ledger, containing all other accounts.

As a business continues to grow, it is found convenient to subdivide the Journal and Ledgers for ease of reference and to enable more clerks to be employed. If the volume of work is too great for one clerk the obvious answer is to obtain another clerk. But they cannot both work in the same book at the same time, so clearly subdivision of the books is a necessity.

Many of a trader's transactions are goods bought on credit for resale. Whenever he buys goods he receives from the seller a document called an *invoice* setting out the quantity, description, price and value of the goods. From the invoice the buyer enters the details into the Journal and so into the Ledger (debit Purchases: credit the supplier's account). Here clearly is an opportunity for subdivision.

A *separate Journal* (variously called the Purchases Journal, Bought Journal, Purchases Book, Purchases Day Book, Bought Day Book) is kept for purchases on credit for resale, and a *separate ledger* called the Bought or Purchases Ledger is kept for the *accounts of suppliers* of these goods. All other Journal entries will continue to be made in the original Journal which can now be called the *Journal Proper*, and all other accounts (except Cash and Bank) will continue to be in the original Ledger which can now be called the *General Ledger*.

It is plain that *all* debits from the Bought Journal must go to the Purchases Account, so there is no need either to make separate individual entries to this account or to show the invoice total in the first money column in the Bought Journal

—*details* of the invoice can be entered there instead (see below for example). In the second money column will be entered the total of each invoice, and this will be posted to the credit side of the supplier's account in the Bought Ledger. At the end of the month, or other convenient time, the Invoice Total column in the Bought Journal can be added up and one large aggregate debit entered in the Purchases Account in the General Ledger.

Below is a worked example. A careful study of this should make the matter clear. The student cannot be expected to have copies of all books of account, so that the usual procedure in the classroom is to put the heading "Bought Journal" at the top of a page in the Journal, and, for the purpose of working exercises, treat that page as a special and separate book.

BOUGHT JOURNAL   46

Date	Particulars	Led. Fol.	Details of Invoice	Invoice Total
			£	£
Mar. 1	*Jacksons, Ltd.—* 6 Oak Dining Tables at £10 each	BL.9		60·00
10	*Furniture Supply Co.—* 3 Walnut, Panelled, 4 ft. 6 in. Bedsteads at £11·50 . .	BL.23		34·50
17	*Hoxton & Sons—* 6 Frameless Mirrors, 18 in. by 12 in., at £0·75 each . .	BL.41		4·50
30	*Artistic Furnishing Co.—* 1 Second-hand Mahogany Writing Table . . . 3 Carved Oak Stools at £2·50 each	BL.27	8·00 7·50	
				15·50
		GL.54		£114·50

This is a short example. In practice, the month's list of purchases may take up several pages. Each page in that case is added and the total carried forward to the top of the next page until the final total for the month is reached. The last item in the example shows two articles bought from the same firm on the same day. The items composing the purchases are entered in the Details column and the total carried into the Invoice Total column. The details column is not added at the foot.

It will be observed that there is *no narration* for each entry in this Journal. The descriptions and details are sufficient. There is no point in stating "Goods bought on credit for resale," since if they were not they would not be in this Journal.

Of course, in business the entries in the Bought Journal are far more numerous than the above example suggests. The items are posted *daily* to the Personal Accounts of suppliers in the Bought Ledger. In classroom practice the student is advised to post each item to the Ledger Account immediately the entry is made in the Bought Journal, so that the Ledger Accounts are kept up to date. Then, if at any time we desire to know how a supplier's account stands, we can be certain that it represents the true state of affairs.

For the above example the Ledger accounts concerned appear as follows—

BOUGHT LEDGER

Dr.				JACKSONS, LTD. (9)			*Cr.*
			£	19.. Mar. 1	Purchases .	BJ.46	£ 60·00

Dr.				FURNITURE SUPPLY CO. (23)			*Cr.*
			£	19.. Mar. 10	Purchases .	BJ.46	£ 34·50

Dr.				HOXTON & SONS (41)			*Cr.*
			£	19.. Mar. 17	Purchases .	BJ.46	£ 4·50

Dr.				ARTISTIC FURNISHING CO. (27)			*Cr.*
			£	19.. Mar. 30	Purchases .	BJ.46	£ 15·50

GENERAL LEDGER

Dr.			PURCHASES ACCOUNT (54)				*Cr.*
19.. Mar. 31	Total Credit Purchases for March . .	BJ.46	£ 114·50				£

The Bought Journal is a list of purchases on credit in the order in which they happen.

Some traders, particularly those with an adding machine, may simply make a list of the total amounts of each invoice and enter the name of the supplier and the invoice number against each amount. The total of the list is posted to the Purchases Account in the General Ledger and then filed. A file of weekly or monthly lists thus constitutes an abbreviated *Purchase Journal. Cash* purchases are *not* included in these lists. When cash is paid for a purchase, the Cash Book is credited and the Purchases Account is debited with the amount of the purchase.

EXERCISE 33

Enter the following purchases on credit in F. Peal & Co.'s Bought Journal—

Feb. 1. Bought from the Hardware Co., Ltd.—
   One dozen galvanized iron garden mats at £0·52 each.
  5. Purchased from Gardiner & Co.—
   4 lawn sprinklers at £1·20 each.
 10. Bought from Walton & Fuller—
   6 rolls of roofing felt, each 25 yd., at £1·50 a roll.
 17. Bought from Martin & Sons—
   3 sack barrows, rubber tyred, at £5·75 each.
 24. Purchased from Gardiner & Co.—
   6 digging forks, 4 prongs, at £0·25 each.
 28. Purchased from Walton & Fuller—
   56 lb. roofing nails, 2 in., at £4·26 per cwt.

(Total, £40·92.)

EXERCISE 34

Enter up Godfrey & Co.'s Bought Journal. Open Ledger accounts, including Purchases Account, and post the items, including total of Purchases Journal—

Mar. 1. Bought from the Wire Netting Co., Ltd.—
   1 roll wire netting 3 in. mesh, 1 yd. wide, at £0·62.
Mar. 10. Purchased from Martin & Holiday—
   6 reels galvanized barbed wire, each ¼ cwt., at £0·85 per reel.
  15. Purchased from Hardy & Co.—
   2 water barrows, 20 gallons, at £3·50 each.
  27. Purchased from London Timber Stores—
   6 lengths wood trellis, 18 in. wide, at £0·20 per piece.

(Total for March, £13·92.)

EXERCISE 35

Carry on the above Bought Journal for month of April and treat as above, using the same Ledger accounts—

Apr. 3. Purchases from Martin & Holiday—
   12 pairs garden shears, 8½ in., at £0·25 per pair.
   3 pairs border shears, 9 in., at £0·45 per pair.
  10. Bought from London Timber Stores—
   12 lengths wood trellis, 2 ft. wide, at £0·27 per piece.
  18. Purchased from Hardy & Co.—
   12 hammock deck chairs at £0·52 each.
   6 hammock deck chairs, with canopy, at £0·77 each.
  28. Purchased from the Wire Netting Co., Ltd.—
   3 rolls wire netting, 2 in. mesh, at £0·75 each.

(Total for April, £20·70.)

EXERCISE 36

Enter the following transactions, using Journal Proper, Bought Journal and double-column Cash Book, and post to the Ledger accounts. Take out Trial Balance.

Wm. Rogerson's position on 1st January was as follows—

	£
Cash in hand	20·30
Cash at bank	148·55
Stock	275·00
Shop fittings	63·50

Jan. 1. Bought from Bush & Co. Ltd.—
   12 doz. table knives at £1 per doz.
   12 doz. table forks at £0·75 per doz.
  4. Bought from Newington & Sons—
   4 doz. leather razor strops, 2 doz. at £0·20 each,
   remainder at £0·15 each.
   Assortment of luggage straps for £6.

8. Cash sales to this date	37·50
Paid cash into bank	50·00

			£
Jan. 15.	Bought new plate glass window shelves, paying by cheque		15·00
	Cash sales to date		39·15
	Paid cash into bank		25·00

Jan. 17. Bought from R. W. Cross—
    4 doz. pairs of scissors, two sizes, at 20p per pair.
    6 sets of carvers at £0·90 per set.
    12 knife sharpeners at 30p each.

Jan. 20. Paid Bush & Co. their account by cheque.

			£
23.	Sundry shop expenses paid in cash		1·55
24.	Sold goods for cash		47·25
28.	Paid assistants' wages in cash . . .		20·00

(Trial Balance totals, £664·25.)

Prepare Trading and Profit and Loss Account and Balance Sheet as at 31st January. Stock in hand at that date, £238.

(Cash Balance, £47·65. Bank Balance, £187·55. Gross Profit, £32·90. Net Profit, £11·35. Balance Sheet totals, £551·70.)

ADDITIONAL EXERCISES

Graded Book-keeping Exercises, Nos, 44 to 48.

CHAPTER XII

THE RETURNS OUTWARDS JOURNAL
AND CREDIT NOTES

IT happens occasionally that of the goods purchased some have been damaged in transit, others are found to be defective or not up to sample. For these or other reasons the goods are returned to the senders. A record of the return of goods purchased on credit is kept in a Returns Outwards Journal (or Purchases Returns Journal) in which the ruling and method of entry are similar to those of the Bought Journal.

Take the following transactions arising out of the purchase mentioned in the preceding chapter—

Mar. 19. Returned to Hoxton & Sons, two of the frameless mirrors purchased on 17th Mar. wrong size delivered.

We should enter this in our Returns Outwards Journal thus—

RETURNS OUTWARDS JOURNAL   14

Date	Particulars	Led. Fol.	Details of Credit Note	Credit Note Total
			£	£
19.. Mar. 19	*Hoxton & Sons—* Two Frameless Mirrors at £0·75 each, wrong size delivered .	41		1·50

Note that "narrations" in this Journal consist of details of the goods being returned with some explanation of the reason for their return—in this case "wrong size delivered."

The original purchase was credited to Hoxton & Sons'
account in the Bought Ledger. The returns item is now posted
from the Returns Journal to that account, which should now
appear as below—

BOUGHT LEDGER

Dr.				HOXTON & SONS (41)			Cr.
19.. Mar. 19	Returns .	.	ROJ. 14	£ 1·50	19.. Mar. 17	Purchases .	BJ.46	£ 4·50

The double-entry in the Ledgers for the returns outwards is
completed periodically by the monthly (or other agreed period)
total of the Returns Outwards Journal being transferred to
the credit of the Purchases Account. The balance of the
Purchases Account at the close of the trading period is the net
total of purchases for that period that is required for the
Trading Account. Assuming the above returns to be the total
for March, the Purchases Account shown in the preceding
chapter should now appear thus—

GENERAL LEDGER

Dr.				PURCHASES ACCOUNT (54)				Cr.
19.. Mar. 31	Total Credit Purchases for March .	.	PJ.46	£ 114·50	19.. Mar. 31	Total Returns for March	.	ROJ. 14	£ 1·50

Credit Notes

For this return of goods Hoxton & Sons would credit our
account in *their* Ledger and send to us a Credit Note, which
is a printed document that states that our account has been
duly credited and giving the amount and the reason. We
could ourselves send a debit note, a form stating that Hoxton
& Sons' account in our Ledger has been debited with the
stated sum and giving the reason for the debit. But debit
notes are seldom used for this purpose. It is more usual to
write notifying that the goods are being returned and asking,

Telegrams: WISCO, CITY, LONDON.
Telephone: EAST 3950 (4 lines).

No. B.C.....1467....

44 LONDON ROAD,
LONDON, E.C.2
1*st July*, 19..

Messrs. Wilson & Smith,
Oliver Road,
Wokingham.

CREDITED BY
THOMAS GODFREY & SONS, LTD.

		£
June 29	*Two Cases returned, invoiced to you on* 12*th June,* *Invoice No.* 2346	1·25

SPECIMEN CREDIT NOTE

at the same time, for a credit note to be forwarded. Entries in the Returns Outwards Journal are made from credit notes.

In classroom work a page in the Journal is headed "Returns Outwards Journal" as representing the separate book which would be in use in actual practice.

To conclude this chapter, it may be pointed out that instead of the totals of the Returns Outwards Journal being credited to the Purchases Account, they may be posted to the credit of a Returns Outwards Account in the General Ledger. In preparing the Trading Account at the close of the trading period the balance of the Returns Outwards Account is transferred to the Trading Account, but not to the credit side as theoretically it should be. As the net purchases for the year are wanted the returns are shown as a deduction from the purchases on the debit side of the account. For example—

Dr.   TRADING ACCOUNT (Debit Side Only)

19..		£	£
	Purchases	114·50	
	Less Returns	1·50	113·00

Both methods of posting the returns are acceptable, but the student is advised to use the latter method.

The student can now work with 3 Journals and 3 Ledgers.

EXERCISE 37

Enter the following items in F. Peal & Co.'s Returns Outwards Journal—

Feb. 6. Returned to Gardiner & Co.—

2 lawn sprinklers at £1·20 each, damaged in transit.

12. Returned to Walton & Fuller—

1 roll of roofing felt at £1·50 per roll—short length of roll received.

19. Returned to Martin & Sons—

3 sack barrows at £5·75 each.

Rubber tyred barrows ordered but not received.

26. Returned to Gardiner & Co.—

1 digging fork at £0·25—not of kind ordered.

(Total, £21·40.)

EXERCISE 38

Post the above items, including the total of the Returns Outwards Journal, to their appropriate Ledger accounts.

EXERCISE 39

M. Murphy's position on 1st December was as follows—

	£
Cash in hand	30·10
Cash at bank	144·70
Stock	285·00
Shop fittings	57·25
Owing to V. Brown & Sons	39·20

Enter the following transactions, using Journal Proper, double-column Cash Book, Purchases Journal, and Returns Outwards Journal, and post to the Ledger accounts. Take out Trial Balance—

	£
Dec. 4. Cash sales	48·60

8. Purchased from Barker & Robinson—

6 picnic cases for two persons at £1·25 each.

6 picnic cases for four persons at £1·50 each.

4 combined tea and luncheon baskets at £2·75 each.

9. Paid cash for stationery . . . . . 1·50

11. Returned to Barker & Robinson—

2 picnic cases at £1·50 each. Received in damaged condition.

14. Cash sales . . . . 52·80

Paid cash into bank . . . . . . 80·00

19. Bought from V. Brown & Sons—

3 croquet sets at £3·50 each.

6 Badminton racquets at £1·60 each.

			£
Dec.	21.	Cash sales	71·00
		Paid cash into bank .	70·00
		Returned to V. Brown & Sons—	
		1 Badminton racquet at £1·60—defective stringing.	
	24.	Paid sundry Christmas boxes in cash .	8·00
	28.	Paid V. Brown & Sons their account by cheque.	
	29.	Cash sales	66·00
	30.	Paid cash into bank .	80·00
	31.	Paid rent of shop by cheque	16·00

(Trial Balance totals, £745·35.)

Prepare Trading and Profit and Loss Account and Balance Sheet as at 31st December. Stock in hand at that date, £184.

(Cash Balance, £29·00. Bank Balance, £301·00. Gross Profit, £94·40. Net Profit, £68·90. Balance Sheet totals, £571·25.)

ADDITIONAL EXERCISES

Graded Book-keeping Exercises, Nos. 49 to 52.

CHAPTER XIII

THE SALES JOURNAL AND SALES LEDGER

WE have seen how the book-keeping involved in the purchasing of goods on credit has been separated from the main Journal and Ledger by the use of the Bought and Returns Outwards Journals and the Bought Ledger. A similar subdivision can be made for sales on credit. Of course, not all businesses sell on credit—most shops and restaurants do not. *Occasional* sales on credit will be entered through the Journal Proper as already explained, but where all, or nearly all, sales are made on credit, as with sales by wholesalers to retailers, then it is common-sense to divert such entries into a Sales Journal and to keep the customers' accounts in a separate Sales Ledger.

As sellers of goods we shall send invoices to our customers and the carbon copies of these will be entered by the sales clerks into the Sales Journal, which is ruled and headed in exactly the same way as the Bought Journal.

No "narrations" are made in the Sales Journal for the same reason as for their not appearing in the Bought Journal.

Cash sales will continue to be debited to Cash or Bank and credited to the Sales Account, no Journal entry being required.

The sale of assets such as machinery, office furniture, etc., will continue to be made in the Journal Proper. Look back at the rules for Journal entries.

The customers' accounts should be debited as soon as the copies of the invoices have been entered in the Sales Journal but *one large credit* will be entered in the Sales Account at the end of the month (or other convenient time) in the General Ledger.

The following is a brief illustration of a series of entries in a Sales Book and of the Ledger accounts affected by them.

SALES JOURNAL 29

Date	Particulars	Led. Fol.	Details of Invoice	Invoice Total
			£	£
19.. Mar. 3	E. Needham— 3 Oak Tables at £15·75 each . 3 Adjustable Chairs at £4·20 each . . .	SL.81	47·25 12·60	59·85
10	E. Courtney & Sons— 2 Walnut Bedsteads at £16·80 each . . .	SL.44		33·60
19	W. Goodwin— 12 Frameless Mirrors, 18 in. by 12 in., at £1·25 each .	SL.53		15·00
26	N. Pharaoh & Co.— 3 Oak Tables at £15 each . 3 Oak Carved Stools at £4·20 each . . .	SL.37	45·00 12·60	57·60
		GL.66		£166·05

These items would be posted to the following accounts—

SALES LEDGER

Dr.   E. NEEDHAM (81)   **Cr.**

19.. Mar. 3	Sales . .	SJ.29	£ 59·85				£

Dr.   E. COURTNEY & SONS (44)   **Cr.**

19.. Mar. 10	Sales .	SJ.29	£ 33·60				£

Dr.   W. GOODWIN (53)   **Cr.**

19.. Mar. 19	Sales .	SJ.29	£ 15·00				£

Dr.   N. PHARAOH & CO. (37)   Cr.

19.. Mar. 26	Goods .	.	SJ.29	£ 57·60				£

GENERAL LEDGER

Dr.   SALES ACCOUNT (66)   Cr.

				£	19.. Mar. 31	Total Credit Sales for March .	. SJ.29	£ 166·05

EXERCISE 40

Enter the following sales on credit in Arthur Collins & Sons' Sales Journal—

June 4. Sold to J. Platt & Co.—

        3 gardeners' wheelbarrows, painted, at £4·40 each.

        3 gardeners' wheelbarrows, painted, with loose tops, at £5·25 each.

   11. Sold to Garden Supplies, Ltd.—

        18 brass garden syringe pumps at £3·25 each.

   19. Sold to Maybury & Hill—

        3 hose reels, galvanized, at £1·50 each.

   24. Sold to Brixton Ironmongery Stores—

        3 garden rollers, double cylinders, 14 in. by 14 in., at £4·05 each.

        3 garden rollers, double cylinders, 16 in. by 16 in., at £4·75 each.

   28. Sold to George Smith & Sons—

        1 doz. galvanized iron garden mats at £1·40 each.

        3 lawn tennis court markers at £8·75 each.

        24 quart cans lubricating oil at £0·50 per can.

Open the appropriate Ledger accounts, including Sales Account, and post the above items, including total of Sales Journal to the Sales Account.

(Total, £173·40.)

EXERCISE 41

Carry on the Sales Journal for the month of July and treat as Exercise 40, using the same Ledger accounts—

July 1. Sold to Garden Supplies, Ltd.—

        12 folding garden chairs at £2·40 each.

    9. Sold to Maybury & Hill—

        24 deck chairs, job line, at £1·65 each.

        4 garden seats, 4 ft., at £2·25 each.

   17. Sold to George Smith & Sons—

        2 doz. garden trowels, 6 in., at £2·25 per doz.

   24. Sold to Maybury & Hill—

        6 greenhouse watering cans at £0·50 each.

   30. Sold to J. Platt & Co.—

        6 folding camp stools, steel frames, at £7·80 per doz.

(Total, £88·80.)

EXERCISE 42

H. Lloyd's financial position on 1st January was as follows—

	£
Cash in hand	51·00
Cash at bank	204·17
Stock	225·00
Debtor: L. Fuller (Sales Ledger) . . .	10·50

Enter the following transactions, using double-column Cash Book, Purchases Journal, Purchases Returns Journal, and Sales Journal, and post to the Ledger accounts. Take out Trial Balance—

£

Jan. 2. Purchased from W. Walton—
         3 "Extensor" wireless sets at £15 each.
         3 cabinet gramophones at £18 each.
      6. Sold to L. Fuller—
         2 silk lampshades at £2·60 each.
         1 mahogany lamp standard at £7·35.
     10. Sold to P. Martin—
         1 portable gramophone, £7·50.
         1 portable wireless set, £32.
     12. Paid W. Walton's account by cheque.
     14. Cash sales to date . . . . 64·50
     20. Bought from G. Smith & Co.—
         Job lot of parchment lampshades for £12.
         6 silk pendant shades at £2·01 each.
     21. Returned to G. Smith & Co.—
         2 lampshades at £2·01 each, damaged through faulty
           packing.
     25. Cash sales . . . . 45·00
         Paid cash into bank . . . . . . 120·00
     28. P. Martin paid his account by cheque.
     29. Paid sundry expenses in cash . . . . . 3·15
     30. Paid rent by cheque . . . . 12·60

(Trial Balance totals, £676·28.)

Prepare Trading and Profit and Loss Account and Balance Sheet as at 31st January. Stock on hand, £239.

(Cash Balance, £37·35. Bank Balance, £252·07. Gross Profit, £56·51. Net Profit, £40·76. Balance Sheet totals, £551·47.)

ADDITIONAL EXERCISES

Graded Book-keeping Exercises, Nos. 53 to 57.

CHAPTER XIV

THE RETURNS INWARDS JOURNAL

CUSTOMERS may not always be completely satisfied with the goods sold to them. As discussed in Chapter XII, we may find it necessary to return goods purchased. Similarly, customers may expect us to take back goods previously sold to them because they are not of the kind ordered, or because they have been damaged in transit or are faulty in construction. Whatever the reason, it is as well to oblige customers and take back the articles in order to retain their goodwill, though in many instances they cannot legally enforce it.

The return of goods previously sold on credit is recorded in the Returns Inwards Journal. The ruling and method of entry is the same in this instance as in the case of the Purchases and other books discussed in the three preceding chapters. A separate Returns Inwards Journal is used in business, but in the classroom the student must again use the Journal and set apart a page or so of it and write the heading "Returns Inwards Journal" to represent the special book.

On entry in the Returns Inwards Journal the item should be posted to the credit of the account of the customer who returned the goods. He has parted with the value to us and thereby lessens the sum due from him. The other entry required to complete the double-entry should be on the debit side of the Ledger, but is not made until the Returns Inwards Journal is added for the month. When the total of the returns for that period is known, it is posted to the debit of the Sales Account, which will then show the net sales for the period.

By way of illustration, let us assume that on 7th March E. Needham returned one adjustable chair sold to him on

3rd March (see preceding chapter) as of faulty construction.
This would be entered in the Returns Inwards Journal and
the amount posted to his credit as below—

RETURNS INWARDS JOURNAL   28

Date	Particulars	Led. Fol.	Details of Credit Note	Credit Note Total
19.. Mar. 7	E. Needham— One Adjustable Chair at £4·20— faulty construction . . .	81	£	£ 4·20

The remarks made in Chapter XII concerning "narrations"
in the Returns Outwards Journal apply equally to the Returns
Inwards Journal.

SALES LEDGER

Dr.   E. NEEDHAM (81)   Cr.

19.. Mar. 3	Goods . .	SJ.29	£ 59·85	19.. Mar. 7	Returns .	RIJ. 28	£ 4·20

The Sales Account would appear as follows—

GENERAL LEDGER   66

Dr.   SALES ACCOUNT   Cr.

19.. Mar. 31	Total Returns for March .	RIJ. 28	£ 4·20	19.. Mar. 31	Total Credit Sales for March .	SJ.29	£ 166·05

Instead of debiting Sales Account, the totals from the
Returns Inwards Journal may be posted to the debit of a
Returns Inwards Account in the General Ledger, and this
course is recommended; but in preparing the Trading Account,
as the net Sales figure is wanted, the balance of the Returns
Inwards Account is shown as a deduction from the total sales

for the trading period. This is shown in the following example of the credit side of the Trading Account.

TRADING ACCOUNT (Credit Side Only) *Cr.*

19.. Mar. 31	Sales . . . . . . Less Returns	£ 166·05 4·20	£ 161·85

Reference was made in Chapter XII to the Credit Note. The return inwards just dealt with has been credited to E. Needham's account as he parted with goods value £4·20. In practice, we should send him a credit note to inform him that his account in our Ledger has been credited and stating the amount. The transaction, had it appeared in an examination test, would have been expressed somewhat as follows—

> Mar. 7. E. Needham returned one adjustable chair, £4·20, sold to him on 3rd inst.; construction faulty. Forwarded to him credit note for £4·20.

EXERCISE 43

Enter the following items in the Sales Returns Journal of Arthur Collins & Sons—

June 7. J. Platt & Co. returned as damaged—
　　　　1 gardener's wheelbarrow at £4·40.
　　21. Maybury & Hill returned—
　　　　3 hose reels at £1·50 each as of unsuitable pattern.
　　29. Brixton Ironmongery Stores returned—
　　　　1 garden roller, 16 in. by 16 in., at £4·70, cracked in transit.
　　30. George Smith & Sons returned—
　　　　24 cans lubricating oil at £0·45 per can as not ordered by them.
Post the above items, including the total of the Returns Inwards Journal, to the appropriate Ledger accounts.

(Total, £24·40.)

EXERCISE 44

L. M. Wilkinson's position on 1st September was as follows—

						£
Cash in hand	.	.	.	.	.	31·50
Cash at bank	.	.	.	.	.	312·20
Stock .	.	.	.	.	.	710·00
Shop fittings	.	.	.	.	.	50·00

Open his books of account and enter the following transactions, using the double-column Cash Book, Purchases, Sales, Returns Outwards and

Returns Inwards Journals, and post to the Ledger accounts. Take out Trial Balance—

£

Sept. 4. Bought from E. Wise & Sons—
3 Bergere suites at £90 each.
7. Sold to R. Underhill—
Oak dining-room suite at £78·75.
Oak dining table at £30·60.
12. Sold to M. Cribb—
5 ft. oak sideboard at £40.
3 fireside chairs at £6·30 each.
14. M. Cribb returned—
1 fireside chair at £6·30, upholstery defective.
18. Sold goods for cash . . . . . . 47·50
19. Bought from Johnson & Smith—
3 hall wardrobes in oak at £18 each.
4 gramophone tables at £5·20 each.
20. Paid sundry expenses in cash . . . . 5·70
21. Returned to Johnson & Smith—
2 gramophone tables at £5·20, as faulty.
23. R. Underhill paid his account by cheque.
24. Sold goods for cheque . . . . . 56·60
30. Paid Johnson & Smith their account by cheque.
30. Paid salaries by cheque . . . . . 40·00

(Trial Balance totals, £1,656·45.)

Prepare Trading and Profit and Loss Accounts and Balance Sheet as at 30th September. Stock on hand at that date, £948.

(Cash Balance, £73·30. Bank Balance, £373·75. Gross Profit, £169·65.
Net Profit, £123·95. Balance Sheet totals, £1,497·65.)

ADDITIONAL EXERCISES

Graded Book-keeping Exercises, Nos. 58 to 61.

CHAPTER XV

CLASSIFICATION OF ACCOUNTS

AT this stage students will have realized that, whereas in a very small business all accounts can be kept in one Ledger, in larger organizations several Ledgers may be needed to contain them. The General Ledger, Cash Book, Bought Ledger and Sales Ledger have all been described.

All accounts, in whatever Ledgers kept, can be classified as (1) Personal Accounts—those standing in the names of persons and organizations with whom the business trades, i.e. suppliers and customers; and (2) Impersonal Accounts—covering all other accounts. Impersonal Accounts can be further subdivided into (a) Real Accounts—accounts of real things such as machinery, stock, and cash; and (b) Nominal Accounts, recording expenses, losses and gains, such as rent, carriage, salaries, and interest received.

Sometimes asset accounts (real accounts) and accounts of a private nature, e.g. Capital Account, Drawings Account, Profit and Loss Accounts, etc., are kept in a separate *Private Ledger*, leaving the expenses, losses and gains to be kept in a separate *Nominal Ledger*. No General Ledger would then be required.

The following diagram is an attempt to show the relationship of all the Ledgers and Journals dealt with so far.

Further Remarks Concerning the Trading and Profit and Loss Account

The purpose of the Trading Account is to show the Gross or Trading Profit, that is, the profit made on buying and selling. The purpose of the Profit and Loss Account is to show the net or actual profit of the business by adding to the Gross Profit

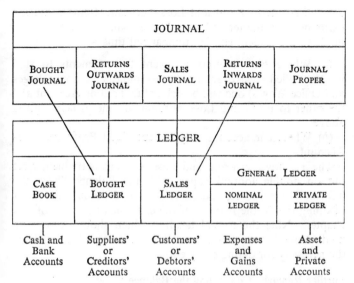

JOURNAL				
BOUGHT JOURNAL	RETURNS OUTWARDS JOURNAL	SALES JOURNAL	RETURNS INWARDS JOURNAL	JOURNAL PROPER

LEDGER				
CASH BOOK	BOUGHT LEDGER	SALES LEDGER	GENERAL LEDGER	
			NOMINAL LEDGER	PRIVATE LEDGER

Cash and Bank Accounts	Suppliers' or Creditors' Accounts	Customers' or Debtors' Accounts	Expenses and Gains Accounts	Asset and Private Accounts

brought down from the Trading Account any gains not directly attributable to trading, e.g. Cash Discount Received (see next chapter), and by deducting all expenses of the business not directly attributable to trading. Where expenses *are* attributable to trading they will have been included in the Trading Account.

Thus, carriage on purchases (Carriage Inwards) is a *Trading Expense* and must be transferred to the Trading Account, since no one would pay carriage on goods bought if they could obtain similarly priced goods of the same quality without paying such carriage. In other words it is an addition to the cost of the goods. On the other hand it is generally expected that the seller will pay carriage on goods sold to customers, so Carriage Outwards is to be regarded as an ordinary expense and will be debited to Profit and Loss Account.

Similarly, the wages of the production or sales staff are an expense directly chargeable against Trading, whilst the salaries of administrative staff, as *not* directly affecting trading results, are chargeable to Profit and Loss Account. Some confusion exists in using the terms "wages" and "salaries" and a useful guide to the student can be summarized thus—

(a) Where *two* accounts are kept for payments to staff whether called wages or salaries (for example, Warehouse Wages and Office Wages) one will be debited to Trading Account and the other to Profit and Loss Account, on the principle given above.

(b) Where *one* account only is kept, debit Profit and Loss Account.

The Trading and Profit and Loss Account is frequently set out on double Journal paper, with the Balance Sheet, for information purposes, and students should get into the habit of doing this in the manner of the example at the end of this chapter. Note the formal heading which should *always* be used. Note that the date appears *in the heading*, which obviates the necessity for dating every entry.

Further Remarks Concerning the Balance Sheet

It has been said in an earlier chapter that the Balance Sheet is a list of balances left in the Ledgers *after* the Trading and Profit and Loss Account has been done. The student should now be sufficiently familiar with the work of extracting a Balance Sheet to be able to set it out in the form of the example which follows. In studying the example, the following should be borne in mind—

(a) Fixed assets are the same from one accounting period to the next, though additions through purchase, and losses through depreciation in value (see Chapter XIX) should be taken into account where appropriate.

(b) Current assets are always changing, always fluctuating, and are *never* the same for every accounting period, e.g. cash becomes stock, stock becomes debtors, and debtors become cash.

(c) Expenditure in advance (explained in Chapter XX).

(d) Long-term liabilities are those which are not payable

until some future date, sometimes unspecified and often many years ahead.

(*e*) Current liabilities are those which are payable at once or in the near future, and include bank overdrafts and payments for expenses accrued due (see Chapter XX) as well as creditors for goods supplied.

TRADING AND PROFIT AND LOSS ACCOUNT OF W. WRIGHT
For the Month Ended 31st January, 19..

	£	£		£	£
Stock .		2,500	Sales . . .	20,750	
Purchases . .	11,000		*Less* Returns .	580	
Less Returns .	170				20,170
		10,830	Stock . . .		2,100
Wages . . .		3,900			
Carriage Inwards .		320			
Gross Profit . . c/d		4,720			
		£22,270			£22,270
Salaries . . .		940	Gross Profit . . b/d		4,720
Rent . . .		600	Rent received .		60
Rates . . .		300	(Sublet premises)		
General Expenses .		1,200			
Carriage Outwards .		420			
Net Profit (transferred to Capital) . .		1,320			
		£4,780			£4,780

BALANCE SHEET OF W. WRIGHT
As at 31st January, 19..

Liabilities	£	£	Assets	£	£
Capital . . .	10,800		FIXED ASSETS—		
Add Net Profit .	1,320		Goodwill, Patents, and Trade Marks .		1,000
	12,120		Land and Buildings .		6,000
Less Drawings .	1,440		Plant and Machinery .		2,800
		10,680	Furniture and Fittings		750
Loan Account . .		5,000	Motor Vehicles .		1,600
Sundry Creditors .		2,000	CURRENT ASSETS—		
Payments accrued due .		88	Sundry Debtors .		1,800
			Stock in hand .		2,100
			Cash at Bank .		1 650
			Cash in hand .		28
			Rates in advance .		40
		£17,768			£17,768

CHAPTER XVI

CASH DISCOUNT AND THE THREE-COLUMN CASH BOOK

To induce customers to pay promptly, traders usually offer an allowance off the sum due if payment is made within a stated period from the date of purchase. Such an allowance is called Cash Discount, and the time allowed for payment is known as the period of credit. The terms of payment are usually printed on the invoice or else stated in a letter at the time of purchase. The invoice may state—

$3\frac{3}{4}$ per cent .   .   .   . 7 days
$2\frac{1}{2}$ per cent .   .   .   . 1 month

Assuming the invoice is for £100, if payment is made within seven days from the date on the invoice £96·25 would be accepted in full settlement of the debt of £100. Likewise, if payment was delayed beyond the seven days but was made within one month, £97·5 would settle the debt. After one month had elapsed the full amount only (£100) would be accepted. Firms making large purchases and paying promptly reap considerable benefit, and at the same time the selling firm has, at a small loss, obtained payment, and with it the opportunity to use the money to finance further business.

Examples

1. We owe Jones & Co. £20 for goods supplied to us on 1st March. Their terms of payment are 5 per cent discount for payment within one month. We pay the account by cheque on 15th March.

2. Thomas & Sons owe us £30 for goods sold to them on 1st March. Our terms are $3\frac{3}{4}$ per cent discount for payment within 7 days, $2\frac{1}{2}$ per cent if within one month. They pay by cheque on 6th March.

Now in our Ledgers these personal accounts should appear on 1st March as shown on p. 83.

BOUGHT LEDGER

Dr.				JONES & CO.			Cr.
			£	19.. Mar. 1	Purchases .	BJ	£ 20·00

SALES LEDGER

Dr.				THOMAS & SONS			Cr.
19.. Mar. 1	Sales . .	SJ	£ 30·00				£

As both payments are made within the time allowed for discount we should—

- (a) *Credit* Bank, £19, paid to Jones & Co. on 15th March.
  Debit Jones & Co.'s account, £19.
- (b) *Debit* Bank, £28·87, received from Thomas & Sons on 6th March.
  Credit Thomas & Sons' account, £28·87.

The personal accounts should now appear thus—

Dr.				JONES & CO.			Cr.
19.. Mar. 15	Bank .	. CB.20	£ 19·00	19.. Mar. 1	Purchases .	BJ	£ 20·00

Dr.				THOMAS & SONS			Cr.
19.. Mar. 1	Sales .	. SJ	£ 30·00	19.. Mar. 6	Bank .	. CB.20	£ 28·87

Obviously the accounts cannot remain like this, for they show that we owe Jones & Co. £1, and Thomas & Sons owe us £1·13. The discount, therefore, is entered, as this has the effect of equalizing the two sides and showing the account as settled. The double-entry is completed by opening Discount Accounts in the Ledger: one for *Discount Allowed* to which is debited the £1·13 which we have *allowed* Thomas & Sons and one for *Discount Received* to which is credited the £1 discount we have *received* from Jones & Co.

BOUGHT LEDGER

Dr.				JONES & Co.			*Cr.*
19.. Mar. 15	Bank . Discount .	.	CB.20	£ 19·00 1·00	19.. Mar. 1	Purchases .	BJ	£ 20·00

SALES LEDGER

Dr.				THOMAS & SONS			*Cr.*
19.. Mar. 1	Sales .	.	SJ	£ 30·00	19.. Mar. 6	Bank . Discount .	. CB.20	£ 28·87 1·13

GENERAL LEDGER

Dr.			DISCOUNT ALLOWED ACCOUNT				*Cr.*
19.. Mar. 6	Thomas & Sons .	.	£ 1·13				£

Dr.			DISCOUNT RECEIVED ACCOUNT				*Cr.*
			£	19.. Mar. 15	Jones & Co.		£ 1·00

The Discount Accounts are nominal accounts. The items on the debit side represent losses, those on the credit side represent gains. The balances of the accounts are transferred to the Profit and Loss Account at the close of the trading period. Some firms prefer to have one account for discounts. If this is done the balance of the account is transferred to the debit or credit side of the Profit and Loss Account and represents the amount by which the discounts allowed exceed the discounts received, or vice versa.

Three-column Cash Book

In practice, it is unusual to enter separately in the Discount Account in the Ledger each item of discount received or allowed. Just as the Sales Journal and Purchases Journal relieve the Sales Account and Purchases Account respectively of separate entries for each transaction, so the use of additional columns in the Cash Book relieves the Discount Accounts of detailed entries. These additional columns, though they have the appearance of account columns, are to be regarded as memoranda only. From them we can obtain periodical totals to enter in the Discount Accounts. The moment these totals are entered up we shall have completed the double-entry in the Ledger for the discounts.

On p. 86 is an example of a three-column Cash Book based upon the following transactions. Note that only the Cash Book entries are shown.

Mar. 1. Cash in hand, £22. Cash at bank, £140·50.
       3. W. Johnson paid his account for £12 by cheque, *less* 5 per cent discount.
       4. Paid P. Brown his account for £10, *less* 2½ per cent.
      6. Thomas & Sons paid their account for £40 by cheque, *less* 3¾ per cent.
      8. Bought for cheque, goods, £20.
    15. Paid Jones & Co. by cheque, £19; discount allowed, £1.
    17. Paid E. Jenkins by cheque, £14·25 in full settlement of his account for £15.
    20. Cash sales, £140.
    21. Paid cash into bank, £120.

Note that the discount columns are totalled and not balanced. These are added weekly or monthly at the time the cash columns are balanced and ruled off. The totals of the discount columns are taken to the Discount Accounts in the Ledger and are entered on the *same sides* of these accounts as they are found in Cash Book. For the above example, the Discount Accounts would appear thus—

Dr.				DISCOUNT ALLOWED ACCOUNT			*Cr.*
19.. Mar. 31	Sundry Discounts Allowed	. CB.20	£ 2·10				£

Dr.

CASH BOOK

			Discount	Cash	Bank
19.. Mar. 1	Balance . .	b/d	£	£ 22·00	£ 140·50
3	W. Johnson .	10	0·60		11·40
6	Thomas & Sons	23	1·50		38·50
20	Cash Sales .	38		140·00	
21	Cash . .	c			120·00
			£2·10	£162·00	£310·40
Apr. 1	Balance .	b/d		32·25	257·15

Cr.

			Discount	Cash	Bank
19..			£	£	£
Mar. 4	P. Brown .	19	0·25	9·75	
8	Purchases .	29			20·00
15	Jones & Co. .	4	1·00		19·00
17	E. Jenkins .	31	0·75		14·25
21	Bank . .	c		120·00	
31	Balance . .	c/d		32·25	257·15
			£2·00	£162·00	£310·40

Dr.   DISCOUNT RECEIVED ACCOUNT   Cr.

			£	19.. Mar. 31	Sundry Dis- counts Received .	CB.20	£ 2·00

The Cash Book, including the discounts, would be posted to customer's and supplier's Ledger accounts. Those of Jones & Co. and Thomas & Sons on p. 84 show these postings.

EXERCISE 45

Enter the following transactions in your three-column Cash Book. Balance the book as on 5th January and bring down the balances.

Jan. 1. Cash in office, £15·50, and in bank, £50.
          Received in cash from J. Sutcliffe, £12·50, *less* 4 per cent discount.
       2. Paid by cheque, to R. Smith, £15.
       3. Paid wages, in cash, £17·50.
       4. Received J. Sutcliffe's cheque for £15; banked same day.
       5. Paid, in cash, J. Eccles's account of £4·50, *less* 2 per cent discount.
          Received in cash from Walter Williams, £20.
          Paid into bank, £25.

(Cash Balance, £0·59.   Bank Balance, £75.   Discount received, £0·09.
                  Discount allowed, £0·50.)   (*U.L. & C.I.*)

EXERCISE 46

Enter the following in the Cash Book and balance and bring down the balances as at 6th January—

Jan. 1. Cash balance, £5·50.
          Bank balance, £67.
       2. Received cheque from Thomas Paine & Co., £11·40, discount allowed, £0·60.
          Paid D. Goodwin, by cheque, £17·55, having deducted £0·45 discount.
       3. Received cash, £5, from R. Englefield, in full settlement of his account for £5·40.
       4. Received cheque from K. Marks, £14·25, allowing him £0·75 discount.
          J. Kingsley paid his account (for £20) by cheque, *less* 7½ per cent discount.
       5. Paid T. Hughes, by cheque, £10.
       6. Paid F. Place, by cheque, £8·55, being allowed £0·45 discount.
          Paid for postage stamps, cash, £0·50.

(Cash Balance, £10.   Bank Balance, £75·05.   Discount allowed, £3·25.
                  Discount received, £0·90.)

EXERCISE 47

Record the following items in the Cash Book and balance the accounts as at 6th July—

		£
July 1.	Cash in hand	10·00
	Cash at bank	87·50
	Received cash from F. Mills	9·50
	Allowed him discount	0·50
	Paid F. Jones, by cheque	9·75
	Was allowed discount	0·25
2.	Paid sundry expenses in cash	1·35
	H. Evans paid in cash	0·95
	Allowed him discount	0·05
3.	A. Black, who owed £20, paid his account by cheque, deducting 5 per cent discount.	
4.	Bought goods for cash	12·00
5.	Received cheque from W. White	15·20
	Allowed him discount	0·80
6.	Paid J. Jordon, by cheque, in full settlement of my account for £30	28·50

(Cash Balance, £7·10. Bank Balance, £83·45. Discount allowed, £2·35. Discount received, £1·75.)

EXERCISE 48

The financial position of F. L. Lloyd, cutler and silversmith, on 1st December 19.., was as follows—

	£
Cash in hand	10
Cash at bank	100
Fixtures and fittings	150
Stock	500
J. Barnett owed	20
Owing to F. Goldsmith	80

Open his books and enter the following transactions therein—

Dec. 2. Bought on credit from F. Goldsmith—
   12 doz. table knives at £3 per doz.
   3 sets of carvers at £4·50 per set.
  7. Sold for cash, sundry articles, £30.
  9. J. Barnett paid his account by cheque, *less* 5 per cent discount.
  12. Sold on credit to J. Thompson & Sons—
   2 doz. razors at £0·75 each.
   10 pairs of scissors at £0·45 per pair.
  18. Cash sales, £57·50.
   Paid £50 in to bank.
  20. Paid F. Goldsmith's account by cheque, *less* 5 per cent discount.
  24. Cash sales, £60.
  29. Paid in cash, sundry expenses, £5·50.

Dec. 30. Received cheque from J. Thompson & Sons in payment of their account, *less* 5 per cent discount.

Take out Trial Balance.

(Cash Balance, £102.   Bank Balance, £67·35.   Trial Balance totals, £876·47.)

Prepare final accounts as at 31st December, 19...   Stock on hand, £470. (Gross Profit, £90·50.   Net Profit, £89·35.   Balance Sheet totals, £789·35.)

ADDITIONAL EXERCISES

Graded Book-keeping Exercises, Nos. 62 to 68.

CHAPTER XVII

TRADE DISCOUNT

TRADE discount is also a deduction from the full price of goods but it is treated in a completely different way. This is because *trade discount* is granted by a supplier for quite different reasons. Many suppliers, manufacturers and importers, supply goods both to wholesalers *and* retailers or to merchants and industrial consumers. For example, manufacturers of building materials supply goods both to builders' merchants and to building firms. From the manufacturer's point of view, supplying goods to merchants has distinct advantages: merchants may well order in large quantities and at regular intervals; they are likely to have satisfactory arrangements for handling deliveries; and they provide a service by storing a wide range of goods and are willing to supply small quantities to their own customers. It is hardly surprising, therefore, that suppliers are prepared to sell goods to such merchants on very favourable terms. Thus a manufacturer of building materials might offer a 20 per cent trade discount to merchants and require builders to pay the full price.

In other cases a manufacturer or importer may issue a catalogue or price list to many customers and potential customers. Varying rates of trade discount may be offered: perhaps $33\frac{1}{3}$ per cent to a large wholesaler who places regular orders and possibly a lower rate, $12\frac{1}{2}$ per cent, to retailers. To a large extent the trade discount offered is a payment for storage and handling and also offers the merchant a margin for profit. *Trade discount* is therefore given by a supplier either on the basis of quantity or because the customer is in a business of a particular sort. Unlike *cash discount* it is given whether the customer pays promptly or not. Indeed, the student may often find that in certain transactions both a *trade discount* and a *cash discount* are offered. Trade discount will be deducted on the Sales invoice and the customer will be required only to pay the lower (net) amount. He may also earn a cash discount for prompt payment. In both the supplier's and the customer's books the transaction will be entered at the net amount, i.e. price less trade discount. Should the customer subsequently earn the cash discount also, this deduction will be dealt with in the way described in Chapter XVI.

So that the trade discount granted may be on record for reference purposes, a note is made of it in the subsidiary books, but care should be taken that the *net amount only* is posted to the customer's, or supplier's, account. The trade discount is never entered in the Ledger.

Example

Mar. 1. Motor Spares Co. sold to P. Gascoigne & Sons 12 sheets 54 in. by 48 in. transparent celluloid at £0·75 per sheet, *less* 20 per cent trade discount.

The Motor Spares Company would record this as follows—

SALES JOURNAL 23

Date	Particulars	Led. Fol.	Details of Invoice	Invoice Total
			£	£
19.. Mar. 1	*P. Gascoigne & Sons—* 12 Sheets 54 in. by 48 in. Celluloid, at £0·75 per sheet . . . *Less* 20 per cent Trade Discount . . .	29	9·00 1·80	7·20

Should Gascoigne & Sons return two sheets because they were defective, Motor Spares Company would make the following entry in the Returns Inwards Journal.

RETURNS INWARDS JOURNAL   9

Date	Particulars	Led. Fol.	Details of Credit Note	Credit Note Total
19.. Mar. 5	*P. Gascoigne & Sons—* 2 Sheets Celluloid at £0·75 each— defective . . . . *Less* 20 per cent Trade Discount	29	£ 1·50 0·30	£ 1·20

Obviously, if the net price per sheet is £0·60, Gascoigne & Sons can receive £0·60 credit only for each sheet returned. Many students forget to deduct trade discount from the returns where it was deducted in the original sale or purchase.

P. Gascoigne & Sons' account in Motor Spares Company's Ledger would appear thus.

SALES LEDGER

Dr.   P. GASCOIGNE & SONS   *Cr.*

19.. Mar. 1	Sales . .	SJ.23	£ 7·20	19.. Mar. 5	Returns . .	RIJ.9	£ 1·20

Note that the net amounts only have been posted.

Purchases subject to trade discount would be entered in a similar way in the Purchases Journal and the net amount credited to the seller's personal account. Returns of such purchases would be entered in the Returns Outwards Journal, care being taken to deduct the percentage of trade discount allowed on the original purchase.

EXERCISE 49

Enter the following transactions in the Sales and Purchases and Returns Journals of Arthur Wareham & Co., merchants—

June   1. Bought from Star Steel Co.—
       6 weed eradicators at £0·50 each, *less* 20 per cent trade discount.

June 3. Bought from Johnson & Bates—
    1 doz. lawn rakes, flexible teeth, at £1·30 each, *less* 25 per cent trade discount.
  5. Sold to Pringle & Nash—
    4 garden incinerators, at £2·75 each.
    4 refuse destructors, corrugated steel, at £4 each.
    All *less* 10 per cent trade discount.
  7. Sold to Watson & Sons—
    2 doz. digging trowels.
    2 doz. weeding forks.
    All at £0·45 each, *less* 33⅓ per cent discount.
  10. Returned to Johnson & Bates—
    2 lawn rakes purchased on 3rd June as damaged.
  15. Sold to Pringle & Nash—
    6 tree pruners, 12 ft., at £4·60 each, *less* 20 per cent trade discount.
  17. Pringle & Nash returned one refuse destructor sold to them on 5th June as damaged in transit.

(Totals: Purchases Journal, £14·10; Sales Journal, £60·78; Returns Outwards, £1·95; Returns Inwards, £3·60.)

EXERCISE 50

The financial position of T. Burns, a furniture dealer, on 1st January, 19.., was as follows—

		£
Cash in hand	.	22
Cash at bank	.	295
Fixtures and fittings	.	280
Stock	.	720
J. Johnson owed	.	50
Owing to F. Naylor	.	110

Journalize these opening entries, and from the following transactions enter up the Cash Book (three columns), Purchases Journal, Sales Journal, and Returns Journal. Post all the items into the Ledger and draw out a Trial Balance and prepare a Trading Account, Profit and Loss Account, and Balance Sheet. Balance off the Cash Book—

19..

Jan. 2. J. Johnson paid by cheque the amount due from him, *less* 5 per cent cash discount. Paid the cheque into the bank on the following day.
  3. Sold to L. Lister: 56 chairs at £3·60 each; 12 oak tables at £8 each; and 3 bedroom suites at £55 each (15 per cent trade discount was allowed on the total order).
  5. Purchased from F. Naylor: 10 book-cases at £8·40 each; 10 suites of furniture at £63 each; and sundry job lots for £36 (15 per cent trade discount was allowed on the total order).
  6. Bought by cheque a new show-case costing £75.

Jan.   7. Drew and cashed a cheque for £25 for office expenses, out of
           which the following payments were made: salaries £10, and
           rent £6.
        9. L. Lister returned as damaged 4 chairs sold to him on the 3rd inst.
       11. Remitted F. Naylor a cheque for £150.
       12. Cash sales to date, £125, out of which £100 was paid into the bank.

Trial Balance totals, £2,372·71.

Stock on hand on 14th January, 19.., £875.

(Gross Profit, £23·47. Net Profit, £4·97. Balance Sheet totals, £1,859·47.)

(U.E.I.)

EXERCISE 51

Henry Goodman is in business as a gentlemen's outfitter. The following
balances apppeared in his books on 30th June, 19..—

		£
Stock .		240·63
Cash in hand		15·50
Cash at bank		374·40
Furniture and fittings .		176·37
Sundry Debtors: J. Bright		56·16
H. Small		11·44
J. Davis		115·00
Sundry Creditors: R. Darnley		75·10
T. Hope		162·40
Capital		752·00

Enter the above balances in the Journal and post them to the Cash Book and
appropriate Ledger accounts. Record the following transactions in the subsidiary books and post them to the Ledger. Balance the accounts and extract
a Trial Balance.

N.B. Trading Account, Profit and Loss Account, and Balance Sheet are *not*
required.

19..

July   1. Drew £20 from bank for office cash.
       2. Purchased, on credit, from the Super Shirt Co.—
             3 doz. cotton shirts at £12·60 per doz.
             5 doz. dress shirts at £2·25 each.
          The whole transaction subject to 10 per cent trade discount.
       6. Purchased, for cash, second-hand show-case, £10.
       9. J. Bright forwarded cheque for £50 on account.
      12. Sold, on credit, to J. Bright—
             6 doz. handkerchiefs at £1·25 per doz.
      14. Paid, in cash, wages, £7·50.
      15. Withdrew, by cheque, £15 for private purposes.
          Sundry cash sales, £12.
      16. J. Bright returned 2 doz. handkerchiefs as imperfect.
      17. Paid rent, by cheque, £4·50.
      18. Purchased, on credit, from the Super Shirt Co.—
             4 doz. collars at £0.55 per doz.

July 20. Returned 1 doz. collars, purchased on 18th inst., not as ordered
£0·55.

J. Davis paid his account by cheque and he was allowed 2½ per cent
discount.

23. Paid for new safe, by cheque, £75.

26. Sold, on credit, to J. Bright—
4 doz. shirts at £2 each.
6 doz. handkerchiefs at £1 per doz.

28. Sundry cash sales, £18·50.

30. Paid £25 into the bank from office cash.
Forwarded cheque to R. Darnley for £74 (discount £1·10) and
cheque for £130, on account, to the Super Shirt Co.
Paid, in cash, wages, £7·50.

(Trial Balance totals, £1,083·22.)   (*U.E.I.*)

EXERCISE 52

On 1st March, 19.., R. Rose commenced business as a coal and coke
merchant and general carter. On that date he had £620 at the bank, a horse
and cart valued at £295, and 2 motor lorries valued at £1,440. The final
instalment due on these lorries (£20) was still owing to Commercial Motors,
Ltd. G. Dickson owed £65 to R. Rose for carting done for him.

Open the accounts necessary to record the above position in the Ledger, and
post thereto, through the proper subsidiary books, the following transactions—

19..
Mar. 2. Drew and cashed cheque, £30, for petty cash purposes.

3. Paid, by cheque, the amount due to Commercial Motors, Ltd.

5. Purchased, on credit, 75 tons coal from the Coal Board at £6
per ton, *less* 10 per cent trade discount.

8. Paid, by cheque, £16 for carriage.

12. Sold, on credit, to G. McArthur, 5 tons coal at £8 per ton.

14. Paid, in cash: wages, £18·50; office expenses, £4.

16. Purchased, on credit, from F. Farmer, 1½ tons hay at £8·50 per ton.

18. Paid, by cheque, Coal Board amount due *less* 5 per cent cash
discount.

20. G. McArthur paid his account, by cheque, *less* 5 per cent cash
discount. Paid same into bank.

22. Sold, for cash, 5 cwt. of coal at £0·50 per cwt. Paid amount into
petty cash.

25. Sent invoice to E. Wright for carting 30 tons building materials
at £0·75 per ton, and supplying 2 tons of coal at £4 per ton,
less 10 per cent trade discount on the whole invoice.

Balance the Ledger, bring down the balances, and extract a Trial Balance as
on 25th March, 19...

N.B. No Profit and Loss Account or Balance Sheet is to be prepared.

(Trial Balance totals, £2,502·95.)

(*R.S.A.*)

ADDITIONAL EXERCISES

Graded Book-keeping Exercises Nos. 69 to 71.

CHAPTER XVIII

PETTY CASH

When the Cash Book was introduced, it was stated that it is customary to bank all monies received on the day of receipt. It is also usual in business to pay all, or as many as possible, accounts by cheque. The object is to keep money retained on the premises down to the minimum, thus reducing the risk of theft. The cash columns in the two- and three-column Cash Books are, therefore, very little used: money for the small or petty disbursements is obtained from the bank and is frequently given into the charge of a junior clerk. Since the latter will not have control of the Cash Book, the Cash Account which can now be called the *Petty Cash Account* is kept in a separate Petty Cash Book and the main Cash Book which will contain discount columns and bank columns is often called the Bank Cash Book.

The cash columns in the Bank Cash Book are usually retained but given a different function: they supply details of payments into the bank and details, where necessary, of cash cheques drawn out.

Example

Cheques received from W. Green £15·22, T. White £301·57 and Z. Brown £6·30 were all banked on 28th July. On the same day a cheque was drawn for £498·37; £10 of this sum was for Petty Cash, £30 personal drawings for the owner and the rest for wages. These would be entered in a three-column Cash Book as shown on the opposite page.

In this way it is easy to see the total amount banked daily and the total of every cheque paid out, thus making it possible to check the Bank Statements (see Chapter XXVI) as well as making it possible to post to individual accounts—to the

BANK CASH BOOK

	Discount	Details	Bank			Discount	Details	Bank
	£	£	£			£	£	£
19.. July 28				19.. July 28				
W. Green	17·15	15·22		Wages		458·37	
T. White		301·57		Petty Cash		10·00	
Z. Brown		6·30		Drawings		30·00	
			323·09					498·37

credit of Green, White, and Brown and to the debit of Wages, Petty Cash, and Drawings (in the example which has just been given).

The type of expenditure made through the Petty Cash as a rule falls into the following four categories—

1. Postage (including parcels, telegrams, etc.).

2. Stationery—small items as ink, rubbers, special envelopes.

3. Travelling expenses—as railway and omnibus fares, taxis, etc.

4. Sundry items such as window cleaning, typewriter repairs, milk for office teas, etc.; these are often grouped together under the heading of Office or General or Sundry Expenses.

Special categories of Petty Cash expenditure are, of course, found and will be peculiar to a particular business.

When the petty cashier has spent almost all the money, he will ask for a further sum from the chief cashier. It is expected that the petty cashier will obtain receipts for payments he makes. Where bills are not given, as for travelling expenses, the person claiming the money from the petty cashier will fill in a Petty Cash Voucher which is generally countersigned by a responsible official of the business to authorize payment of the item.

It should be noted that the Petty Cash Book is part of the double-entry system. Although it is kept in a separate book under the charge of the Petty Cashier, it is a *Ledger account*. Money received from the Bank is debited to the Petty Cash Accounts (the Bank column in the Bank Cash Book is credited with the same amount). When the Petty Cashier pays out the various sums of money he credits the Petty Cash Book and the corresponding debits are entered in the appropriate Expense Account in the General Ledger.

Analysed or Columnar Petty Cash Book

If the Petty Cash items are fairly numerous it is an advantage to group items of recurring expenditure under headings and post *in total* at the end of suitable periods (a week, a month) to the Expense Accounts (shown at the head of each column) into the General Ledger. In this way, time is saved by making the analysis at the same time as the entry is made in the Petty Cash Book and the General Ledger accounts are not over-burdened with a large number of small items. The number of the columns and the headings will depend on the nature and requirements of the business. A type of analysed Petty Cash Book in common use is given on p. 100. Note that on the extreme right there is a column headed "Sundries." In this column are placed those items which do not belong to any of the analysis columns. For example, the "loan to employee" is not Postage, Stationery, Travelling or a General Expense and so cannot be extended to those columns. Items in the "Sundries" column are posted *individually* hence the folio column to the left of it: items in the analysis columns are posted *in total* to the account named at the head of each column. The folio number appears underneath as in the example given.

The Imprest System

This is a method by which a measure of control is kept of Petty Cash expenditure. At the beginning of a fixed period of time (e.g. a week, a fortnight, a month) the petty cashier is given a fixed sum of money (e.g. £5, £10, £20). At the end of the period the Petty Cash is balanced, the amount in hand checked with the cash box and the amount spent checked with receipts and petty cash vouchers. The bills and receipts are retained by the head cashier and a cheque is given to the petty cashier for the amount spent. This he cashes at the bank so that he starts the new period with the same amount of money as he started the last.

It should be noted that the imprest system can be used with both the simple and the analysed Petty Cash Books and makes no difference whatever to the book-keeper's work. In the worked example on p. 100 the amount received on 1st January was £10. A fortnight later, when the account was balanced, £5·70 had been spent. If this account was kept on the imprest

PETTY CASH BOOK

Amount Received	CB Fol.	Date	Details	Voucher No.	Total	Postage and Telegrams	Stationery	Travelling Expenses	General Expenses	Fol.	Sundries
£					£	£	£	£	£		£
10·00	31	19.. Jan. 1	Bank								
		3	200 × 1p. Stamps	1	2·00	2·00					
		4	Fares to station (taxi)	2	0·37			0·37			
		6	Pencils and nibs	3	0·24		0·24				
		7	Loan to employee (W. Brown)		1·50					GL.88	1·50
		10	Advertisement for staff	4	0·77				0·77		
			Office teas		0·48				0·48		
		13	Bus fares to solicitor's		0·08			0·08			
		14	Parcel to Kay & Co.		0·26	0·26					
					5·70	2·26	0·24	0·45	1·25		1·50
			Balance c/d		4·30	GL.46	GL.31	GL.37	GL.44		
£10·00					£10·00						
4·30		Jan. 15	Balance b/d								

system, a cash cheque for £5·70 would be given to the petty cashier and debited to the account on 15th January, thus enabling him to start his second fortnight with the same sum as he started the first, i.e. £10.

EXERCISE 53

Draw up a Petty Cash Book with analysis columns for the following kinds of petty cash expenditure, viz.: (1) stationery; (2) postages and telegrams; and (3) carriage.

Enter therein the following transactions and bring down the balance as on 6th March, 19.. —

		£
19..		
Mar. 1.	Received from the chief cashier	20·00
	Paid telegram to Liverpool	0·17
	Paid for postages	0·06
3.	Paid carriage on samples sent to Brown & Co. . .	0·66
4.	Paid postages for 2nd, 3rd, and 4th March . .	0·52
5.	Paid stationery bill	6·50
	Paid telegram to Paris	0·52
6.	Paid carriage of goods	0·50

(Balance, £11·07.)   (U.L.C.I.)

EXERCISE 54

What are the advantages, if any, of using a columnar Petty Cash Book?

Rule a suitable Petty Cash Book and enter the following items, showing the balance in hand at 30th June—

June 25. Received from chief cashier for petty cash, £5·50.
  26. Paid for postage stamps, £0·17; tram fares, 4p.
  27. Paid for window cleaning, £0·14; telegram, 16p.
  28. Paid subscription to general hospital, 30p.
  29. Paid for advertisement in trade directory, £0·37; cleaner's wages, £0·50.
  30. Paid electric light account, £2·22; Wholesale Tobacconists' Supply, Ltd., for goods supplied on credit on 1st June, £0·47.

(Balance, £1·13.)   (R.S.A.)

EXERCISE 55

Rule a Petty Cash Book containing columns headed as follows: Postages, Fares, Stationery, Telegrams, Housekeeper.

Enter the following transactions and balance the account weekly—

Jan. 1. Received from cashier for petty cash, £5.
  2. Bought postage stamps, £0·50.
  3. Paid 'bus fares, £0·08; telegrams, £0·42.
  4. Paid for telegrams, £0·30; stationery, £0·75.

Jan.   5. Paid for postage stamps, £0·25.
        6. Paid housekeeper, £2.
        8. Received from cashier cheque to make up the amount of the
           imprest, viz., £5.
        9. Bought postage stamps, £0·50; string, £0·10.
       10. Paid railway fares, £0·15; telegrams, £0·20.
       11. Paid for ink and nibs, £0·15; parcels, £0·10.
       12. Paid for postage stamps, £0·50; envelopes, £0·40.
       13. Paid housekeeper, £2; tram fares, £0·05.

           (Balance: First week, £0·70; Second week, £0·85.)

EXERCISE 56

On 1st June, 19.., T. W. Halstead's assets and liabilities were as follows:
Cash at Bank, £129·42; Debtors: T. White, £27·50; S. Black, £53·00; Stock,
£210·20; Furniture and Fittings, £950; Creditor: W. Ward, £270·12.

Open by Journal the accounts necessary to record the above position in
Halstead's books, and post thereto, using the proper subsidiary books the
following transactions. A Petty Cash Book, having 3 analysis columns for:
(1) Office Expenses, (2) Stationery, and (3) Purchases, is to be used for recording
cash.

June   1. Drew and cashed a cheque for petty cash, £30.
       2. Sold goods on credit to S. Boxmore, £240, *less* 10 per cent trade
          discount.
       3. Received cheque from T. White for amount due *less* 2½ per cent
          cash discount.
       4. Paid from Petty Cash for office window cleaning, £0·75.
       5. Bought on credit from W. Ward goods, £180, *less* 15 per cent
          trade discount.
          Paid from Petty Cash stationery £2·50 and postage £3.
       6. Sold goods on credit to T. White, £90, and to S. Boxmore, £27.
       8. S. Boxmore returned £50 (gross) of goods sold to them on 2nd
          June.
          Halstead drew cheque for private drawings, £20. Paid in cash for
          purchases, £9.
      10. Cash sales (banked) £82·75. S. Boxmore paid his account by
          cheque *less* 5 per cent cash discount.
      11. Cash Sales (banked), £149. Paid in cash: stationery, £3·75,
          purchases, £4; and office expenses, £2·40.
      13. Paid by cheque W. Ward amount due on 1st June, and rent £45.
      14. Bought new filing cabinets for office, £36, from Office Supplies,
          Ltd.

Balance the Cash Book, Petty Cash Book and Ledger accounts, bringing
down the balances, and extract a Trial Balance as on 14th June.
N.B. No final accounts are required.

(Trial Balance totals, £1,853·75.)

ADDITIONAL EXERCISES

Graded Book-keeping Exercises, Nos. 72 to 83.

CHAPTER XIX

DEPRECIATION, RESERVES AND PROVISIONS

DEPRECIATION is a fall in value. In business, most of the fixed assets become less valuable as they are put to use. A machine costing £500 when new may appear in the firm's Balance Sheet at that value, but if it were to appear year after year at the same figure the question would arise whether the Balance Sheet does show the true financial position. The wear and tear in use obviously leads to a fall in value of the machine, and in time it will have to be replaced. Should it be necessary to realize the firm's assets it is unlikely that a used machine will fetch a price as high as its original cost.

Admitting that year by year the machine falls in value, then the loss must be accounted for as an expense of production since the wear and tear is in the process of production. If this expense is not set off against the profits the owner of the business will find one day that his machine must be replaced, and that he has made no financial provision for its replacement.

In order, therefore, that the assets appear in the Balance Sheet at a figure somewhere near their true value, and that proper provision is made for any fall in value to be treated as an *expense*, it is necessary to "provide for depreciation" when the final accounts are prepared.

Assets may depreciate—

(a) Through wear and tear in use as in the case of machinery, furniture and fittings, loose tools, motor vans and lorries.

(b) Through effluxion or passage of time as in the case of leases of factories and other buildings and of patent rights.

(c) Through obsolescence where, for example, a machine

is rendered out of date through the invention of a more efficient machine.

The amount of the depreciation may be ascertained and treated in one of the following ways—

   (i) By revaluation of the asset.
   (ii) By the Straight Line or Fixed Instalment Method.
   (iii) By the Diminishing Balance Method.

The method selected will depend upon circumstances and the kind of asset.

Revaluation

It is necessary in some instances to revalue the asset. Loose tools are made and used in engineering shops for special jobs. Some may never be required again and others are completely used up. Motor lorries and vans lose heavily in value during the first year of use. In these and similar cases the present value is estimated, and the difference between the present and the last valuation or cost price is the amount of depreciation to be taken into account.

The Straight Line or Fixed Instalment Method

By this method equal instalments are written off the value of the asset year by year. The cost of the machine or other asset is known. It is necessary to estimate its probable working life in years as a useful asset. The number of years divided into the cost will give the instalment or amount of depreciation to be written off each year.

Example

A machine, cost price £500, is estimated to last 10 years.

Annual depreciation $= \dfrac{£500}{10} = £50.$

In this example the asset is extinguished at the end of ten years. Should it be estimated to have any value as "scrap" at the end of its useful life, then such value should be allowed for.

Assuming the "scrap" value to be £50, then £450 (£500 less £50) is the total loss by depreciation. Annual loss by depreciation $= \dfrac{£450}{10} = £45$ per annum.

Diminishing Balance Method

By this method a fixed percentage is written off the first cost of the asset, and a similar percentage off the diminishing value of the asset in subsequent years.

Example

A machine costs £500. Depreciation at 10 per cent is to be written off.

First Year.	Cost price	.	.	.	.	.	. £500
	Depreciation at 10%	.	.	.	.	.	50
							£450
Second Year.	Depreciation at 10%	.	.	.	.	.	45
							£405

At the end of ten years the asset will stand in the books at £174, so that a sufficiently high percentage must be used if it is desired to reduce the asset to a low "scrap" figure within a short period.

The diminishing balance method is favoured as the amounts written off become less and less during the later years, when the charges for repairs are likely to increase owing to the age of the machine.

The Depreciation Account

Whichever method is used, the amount of depreciation is credited to the asset account, the balance of which will be the new value for the asset in the Balance Sheet. The debit entry is made in a Depreciation Account, the balance of which is transferred in due course to the debit of Profit and Loss Account.

Examples

The following assets appear in A.B.'s books at cost—

> Motor Lorries, £2,500.
> Machinery and Plant, £4,000.
> Furniture and Fittings, £800.

Depreciation: Motor lorries by revaluation.
Machinery and Plant by 20 per cent on its diminishing value.
Furniture and Fittings by 10 per cent, equal instalments.

Show the assets accounts for two years. The lorries are valued at £1,800 at the close of the first year and £1,500 at the close of the second year.

Dr.   MOTOR LORRIES   *Cr.*

				£				£
Jan. 1	Balance .	.	b/d	2,500	Dec. 31	Depreciation . . Balance .	c/d	700 1,800
				£2,500				£2,500
Jan. 1	Balance .	.	b/d	1,800	Dec. 31	Depreciation . . . Balance .	c/d	300 1,500
				£1,800				£1,800
Jan. 1	Balance .	.	b/d	1,500				

Dr.   MACHINERY AND PLANT   *Cr.*

				£				£
Jan. 1	Balance .			4,000	Dec. 31	Depreciation . . Balance .	c/d	800 3,200
				£4,000				£4,000
Jan. 1	Balance .	.	b/d	3,200	Dec. 31	Depreciation . . . Balance .	c/d	640 2,560
				£3,200				£3,200
Jan. 1	Balance .	.	b/d	2,560				

Dr.   FURNITURE AND FITTINGS   *Cr.*

				£				£
Jan.	1	Balance . .		800	Dec. 31	Depreciation .	c/d	80
						Balance .		720
				£800				£800
Jan.	1	Balance .	b/d	720	Dec. 31	Depreciation .	c/d	80
						Balance .		640
				£720				£720
Jan.	1	Balance .	b/d	640				

Dr.   DEPRECIATION   *Cr.*

			£				£
Dec. 31	Lorries . .		700	Dec. 31	Transfer to		
	Machinery . .		800		Profit and		
	Furniture . .		80		Loss A/c. .		1,580
			£1,580				£1,580
				(Second year)			
Dec. 31	Lorries . .		300	Dec 31	Transfer to		
	Machinery .		640		Profit and		
	Furniture		80		Loss A/c. .		1,020
			£1,020				£1,020

BALANCE SHEET AS AT 31ST DECEMBER, 19.. (1ST YEAR)

			£	£	£
Left-hand side omitted	*Fixed Assets—*				
	Plant and Machinery .	.	4,000		
	Less Depreciation .	.	800		
				3,200	
	Motor Lorries . .	.	2,500		
	Less Depreciation on				
	revaluation . .	.	700		
				1,800	
	Furniture and Fittings	.	800		
	Less Depreciation .	.	80		
				720	
					5,720

It is usual to keep a record of the assets, apart from the accounts, showing their cost, method of depreciation, and the amounts of depreciation from year to year in a Plant Register, etc.

The Journal entries for the first year of the example are shown below. They would be similar for the second year.

The Balance Sheet should disclose the fact that due allowance has been made for depreciation (see p. 107).

JOURNAL

19.. Dec. 31		£	£
	Depreciation	700	
	Motor Lorries		700
	Depreciation on revaluation at this date.		
	Depreciation	800	
	Machinery and Plant . . .		800
	20% depreciation on diminishing value.		
	Depreciation	80	
	Furniture and Fittings . .		80
	Depreciation of 10% per annum of cost.		
	Profit and Loss Account . . .	1,580	
	Depreciation		1,580
	Transfer of depreciation for the year.		

An alternative treatment to the above is to leave the asset at cost but credit all depreciation to a "Provision for Depreciation of Asset Account" (the debit is posted to the Depreciation Account in the normal way). When the Balance Sheet is prepared the balance on the Provision for Depreciation Account is deducted from the balance on the asset account to give the same net figure as before.

If the depreciation of Motor Lorries in the previous example was treated in this way the accounts would appear as on p. 109.

Dr.				MOTOR LORRIES			Cr.
Year 1 Jan. 1	Balance . .		£ 2,500				£

PROVISION FOR DEPRECIATION OF MOTOR LORRIES

			£				£
Year 1 Dec. 31	Balance . .	c/d	1,000	Year 1 Dec. 31	Depreciation .		700
				Year 2 Dec. 31	Depreciation .		300
			£1,000				£1,000
				Year 3 Jan. 1	Balance .	b/d	1,000

BALANCE SHEET AS AT 31ST DECEMBER, 19.. (2ND YEAR)

	£	£
Fixed Assets— Motor Lorries Cost . . . *Less* Provision for Depreciation .	2,500 1,000	1,500

Reserves

It is not prudent to distribute all the profits of a business. Events may occur occasioning special losses for which no provision has been made, and imposing a strain of the financial resources. This may be avoided to some extent if a portion of the profits are retained in the firm. Hence the creation of Reserves. A Reserve in Book-keeping is a reserve of profits, that is, profits withheld from distribution for the purpose of strengthening the general financial position of the firm. A Provision is part of the profit held back for some specific purpose, such as depreciation of assets.

The profits retained by creating a Reserve or withheld by creating a Provision may remain at the disposal of the business as additional working capital. Alternatively, sums retained in this way could be invested outside the business. Thus amounts set aside to a Provision for Depreciation Account could be invested each year to provide a capital sum with which to buy the replacement asset when the existing one has come to the end of its useful life.

With all Reserves and Provisions, including Provision for Depreciation, profit is kept in the business. The profit available for distribution to the owners of the business is lessened by the amount set aside.

This amount may either be set aside as a special fund to replace an asset or may of course be used generally in the business itself, in which case the amount of working capital is increased.

Both *Reserve* and *Provision* Accounts will have credit balances and, as they are permanent or semi-permanent in nature, they will appear in the Balance Sheet. The general rule is that *Reserves* are shown on the left-hand side (Capital and Liabilities) for they are, in effect, part of the owner's capital. *Provisions*, however, are created for a specific purpose and are thus shown as deductions from the asset to which they refer. This is illustrated in the next section.

Provisions for Bad and Doubtful Debts

The total of book debts appears in the Balance Sheet under the heading "Sundry Debtors." Some of the debts may be bad in that they can never be recovered, and others may be of doubtful value. If this is known then the full total of book debts does not represent the true value of the asset.

Bad debts must be written off by crediting the debtor's account, and debiting the Bad Debts Account for eventual transfer to Profit and Loss Account.

A provision is made for the doubtful debts as profits will be diminished in respect of such debts as it is not found possible to realize.

The amount to provide may be ascertained by a review of the debtors' accounts and a calculation made of the actual debts in doubt, or, if the accounts are numerous then, from past experience, a percentage of the outstanding debts may be assumed to be doubtful and a provision in respect of them made accordingly.

Example

Outstanding debtors amount to £10,000 on 31st December. A provision for bad and doubtful debts at 5 per cent on the outstanding total is to be made.

JOURNAL

			£	£
Dec. 31	Profit and Loss Account . . . Provision for Bad and Doubtful Debts . . . . . . 5% Provision upon Sundry Debtors at this date.		500	500

The Profit and Loss Account will be debited and the Provision Account credited with the sum of £500.

Dr.				PROVISION FOR BAD AND DOUBTFUL DEBTS		*Cr.*
		£	Dec. 31	Profit and Loss A/c. . .		£ 500

When the books are closed the credit balance of £500 remains in the Provision Account as above. It is a liability (if all the debtors paid the amount could be written back to the Profit and Loss Account and taken out by the owner), but it is not shown as a separate item on the left-hand side of the Balance Sheet. It is the practice to show it as a deduction from the item of Sundry Debtors on the assets or right-hand side.

	£	£
Sundry Debtors	10,000	
Less Provision	500	
		9,500

Increasing the Provision

In the Trial Balance prepared at the end of the next trading period, the item "Provision for Bad and Doubtful Debts—£500" will appear as the balance of that account. The item

"Sundry Debtors" will also appear, but is unlikely to coincide in amount with the debtors of last year. It will be greater or less. If the Provision of 5 per cent is considered sufficient, then a provision for doubtful debts on the new figure for debtors will require a larger or smaller sum than £500.

Assuming the Sundry Debtors now stand at £15,000, 5 per cent provision would be £750.

£500 is already set aside from last year. Only £250 will be required to be set aside from this year's profits.

It is essential that a given Trial Balance should be examined carefully to see whether a provision already exists, and that this should be taken into account when the new provision is calculated.

Journal entry for the increased provision—

JOURNAL

			£	£

Dec. 31	Profit and Loss Account . . .
	      Provision for Bad and Doubtful Debts
	 Balance of 5% on Sundry Debtors at this
	      date.
			250	250

Dr.				PROVISION FOR BAD AND DOUBTFUL DEBTS			*Cr.*
		£	Dec. 31	Balance . .	b/d	£ 500
				Profit and Loss A/c. .	J	250

Decreasing the Provision

If the Sundry Debtors stood in the second year at £8,000 as against the £10,000 in the above example, and the provision was to be maintained at 5 per cent, then the existing provision of £500 is too large. At 5 per cent on the present figure of £8,000, the provision should be reduced to £400. £100 has therefore to be written back.

JOURNAL

			£	£
Dec. 31	Provision for Bad and Doubtful Debts . Profit and Loss Account . . . Excess provision of 5% on Sundry Debtors written back.		100	100

Dr.				PROVISION FOR BAD AND DOUBTFUL DEBTS			Cr.
			£				£
Dec. 31	Profit and Loss A/c. .	J	100	Dec. 31	Balance . .	b/d	500

The occurrence in a given Trial Balance of an item "Bad Debts" indicates that accounts have been written off to that extent as bad. The item should be taken to the debit of Profit and Loss Account. It could be debited to the Provision for Bad and Doubtful Debts Account, and set against the provision for bad debts and the provision increased by a similar sum by a new provision from profits. If, however, the item is taken direct to Profit and Loss Account the Provision for Bad Debts is unaffected, and simply serves the purpose of adjusting the asset "Sundry Debtors" to its true value.

Should an amount already written off as a bad debt be paid by a debtor, the personal account should not be credited but the sum should be credited to the Bad Debts Account as an unexpected gain.

Provision for Discounts

A student is sometimes asked to create a Provision for Discounts on Sundry Debtors. The reason given is that as some of the debtors are likely to pay promptly and take any cash discount offered, the item Sundry Debtors is to that extent at too large a figure. The provision is usually calculated in the light of past experience at a percentage of the total debtors, and the entries necessary are similar to those for a Provision for Bad and Doubtful Debts. The percentage should be taken on the net value of the debts after deducting the Bad Debts provision, that is, on the good debts only.

Example

The Sundry Debtors at 31st December amount to £10,000. Provide 5 per cent on this amount for bad and doubtful debts and 2½ per cent for discount.

The Bad and Doubtful Debts Provision would be dealt with as explained above.

The Journal entries for the Provision for Discounts are as below—

JOURNAL

		£	£

Dec. 31	Profit and Loss Account . . .
	     Provision for Discounts on Debtors .
	     2½% Provision for Discounts on Sundry
	        Debtors after deduction for Bad Debts.
		237·50	237·50

Dr.		PROVISION FOR DISCOUNTS ON DEBTORS			*Cr.*
		£	Dec. 31	Profit and Loss A/c. .	J	£ 237·50

The Sundry Debtors and the two provisions would appear in the Balance Sheet as follows—

BALANCE SHEET AS AT 31ST DECEMBER, 19..
(Right-hand side only is shown)

Current Assets	£	£	£
Sundry Debtors		10,000·00	
Less Bad Debts Provision . . .	500·00		
Discounts Provision . . .	237·50	737·50	
			9,262·50

A provision for discounts on creditors may also be created by debiting the amount to a Provision for Discounts on Creditors account and crediting the Profit and Loss Account. This provision would appear in the Balance Sheet as a deduction from the item Sundry Creditors on the left-hand side.

EXERCISE 57

In the books of a firm, at 31st December, are the following assets, at cost—

	£
Plant and Machinery . . .	7,500
Office Furniture . .	600

You are required to show the Ledger accounts for these assets and the Journal entries for depreciation as follows—

On Plant and Machinery. 10 per cent per annum on cost.

On Office Furniture. $7\frac{1}{2}$ per cent per annum on cost.

Post the Journal entries and show the assets as they would appear in the Balance Sheet of the firm.

EXERCISE 58

A business buys an electric lighting plant on 1st January, 19.. for the sum of £2,550. The plant is estimated to last 10 years and to have a scrap value at the end of that time of £250. Show how you would deal with this asset in the books of the business at the end of the first year.   (*R.S.A.*)

EXERCISE 59

The following assets were purchased by a firm on 1st January, 19..—

	£
Machinery	2,000
Furniture	200

The machinery is estimated to have a working life of ten years and to have £200 as scrap value at the end of the period.

Give the entries necessary to allow for depreciation of the machinery by equal instalments, and show the accounts as they would appear for three successive years.

Depreciate the furniture by 5 per cent per annum on cost and show two years' accounts only.

EXERCISE 60

The asset, Machinery and Plant, £3,000, is shown on the firm's books at cost price on 1st January, 19... On preparing the final accounts for the year ended 31st December, it is decided to provide for depreciation at 20 per cent per annum on the diminishing balance.

Give the entries necessary to carry this into effect, and show the accounts for a period of three successive years. Include a Provision for Depreciation Account in your answer.

EXERCISE 61

The Loose Tools of an engineering firm stood on the books at 31st December, at £1,200. A revaluation as at that date gave the Loose Tools to be worth £1,500.

Give the entries required to record this information in the books of the firm.

EXERCISE 62

Explain briefly, but as clearly as you can, why it is generally necessary when preparing the accounts of a business to make provision for depreciation of the "fixed assets."

If you know any exceptions to this general rule, mention them and give your reasons.

NOTE. Goodwill is for the purpose of this question, *not* to be regarded as a "fixed" asset.   (*R.S.A.*)

EXERCISE 63

The item, "Sundry Debtors, £4,600," in a firm's Trial Balance includes some debts of doubtful value. It is desired to create a provision of 5 per cent of the total debtors to provide against loss.

Give the entries necessary to record this and show how the item "Sundry Debtors" would appear in the firm's Balance Sheet.

EXERCISE 64

The Sundry Debtors stand at a total of £8,300 at 31st December, and there is an existing provision of £350 for bad debts. Give the Ledger account showing the existing provision and the entries necessary to ensure that the provision now stands at 5 per cent of the present total of Sundry Debtors.

EXERCISE 65

At 31st December the total of Sundry Debtors stood at £4,100, and the existing Bad Debts Provision at £300. The Provision for Bad Debts is to be maintained at 5 per cent of the Sundry Debtors.

Give the entries required to carry this out, and show how the items will stand in the Balance Sheet.

EXERCISE 66

The following particulars are taken from a firm's books—

Last year the Sundry Debtors stood at £3,600.
This year ,,   ,,   ,,   stand at £2,500.
Last year the Bad Debts Provision was £180.
This year ,,   ,,   ,,   ,,   is to be £125.

Show how the reduction in the Provision is recorded in the firm's books.

EXERCISE 67

The Bad Debt Provision of a company on 1st January, 19.., was £56·52. The bad debts during the year amount to £48·19.

It was decided to bring the provision at 31st December, 19.., to £96·50. Show how this is recorded.

(R.S.A.)

EXERCISE 68

The "Sundry Debtors" of a firm amount to £18,240. It is desired to provide a Bad Debts Provision of 5 per cent and a Provision for Discounts on Debtors of 2½ per cent. Set out the item "Sundry Debtors" as it would appear on the Balance Sheet. *(N.C.T.E.C.)*

ADDITIONAL EXERCISES

Graded Book-keeping Exercises, Nos. 84 to 95.

CHAPTER XX

ADJUSTMENTS, OUTSTANDING LIABILITIES, AND PAYMENTS IN ADVANCE

THE purpose of a Balance Sheet is to show a true and correct view of the state of the financial affairs of the firm as at a particular date. It comprises the balances remaining open in the books of account after the Trading and Profit and Loss Accounts have been prepared, but it is very necessary that each item should be carefully considered to see that it represents the actual value at the time. Due regard must be paid, for example, to the proper depreciation of the assets, the valuation of the stock on hand, and to provisions and reserves as already explained. In addition, account must be taken of every liability outstanding. If rent is owing, then to ignore the fact is to set the profits to that extent at too high a figure. The expenses of each trading period should be paid or provided for out of the profits of that period.

Again, certain payments made in one trading period may properly belong, wholly or in part, to the succeeding period. Rates for the ensuing half-year may be paid in October and may cover the period October to March. If the firm's books are closed on 31st December only half the payment made should be set against the profits of the financial year just ended, and the other half should be set against the profits of the succeeding year. In other words, half the rates represents a payment in advance.

In an examination test such outstanding liabilities or payments in advance are given, but appear outside the Trial Balance. It is for the student to take such items into careful consideration when preparing the final accounts.

Any difficulty is lessened if it is borne in mind that all

items for adjustment or otherwise (including stock in hand) appearing *outside* the Trial Balance must be dealt with twice. Such items have not been passed through the books, and they will affect the Trading Account or the Profit and Loss Account *and* the Balance Sheet. The actual Trial Balance items each appear but once in the final accounts.

Outstanding Liabilities

Example

31st December. One quarter's rent (£200) due 25th December remains unpaid.

Half-year's interest at 6 per cent on £5,000 mortgage on freehold premises had not been paid and no entry put through the books in connexion therewith (ignore income tax).

The Rent Account would show that the first three-quarters' rent (£600) had been paid.

The Interest Account would show that the first half-year's interest (£150) had been paid.

If the balances of these two accounts are transferred to Profit and Loss Account as they stand without adjustment, the profits will be stated at a figure higher than it should be by the £200 rent plus £150 interest outstanding. If no adjustment is made, payment during the following trading period will mean that the profits next year will be less by £350 than they should be if each trading period bears the full total of expenses relative to it.

Dr.   RENT   *Cr.*

			£				£
Apr. 5	Cash .		200	Dec. 31	Profit and Loss A/c.		800
July 6	Cash .		200				
Oct. 4	Cash .		200				
Dec. 31	One quarter's rent outstanding .	c/d	200				
			£800				£800
				Dec. 31	Balance (one quarter's rent).	b/d	200

It is necessary therefore to bring such outstanding items into account in the preparation of the final accounts.

The rent outstanding has been debited to the Rent Account, *and* brought down as a credit balance on the new Rent Account for the next period. The double-entry is within the Rent Account. The whole year's rent £800, and not only the three-quarters which would be in the Trial Balance, is transferred to Profit and Loss Account and charged against profits. But the £200 owing is not paid. The credit balance of the Rent Account must be shown in the Balance Sheet on the left-hand side as a current liability. A provision of £200 from profit has, in effect, been made, and is held in the business to meet this liability in due course.

The Journal entry, if required, would be—

JOURNAL

			£	£
Dec. 31	Rent		200	
	Outstanding Rent . . .			200
	One-quarter's rent outstanding.			

When payment is made cash will be credited as usual, and the Rent Account debited, which will have the effect of cancelling the liability.

The second item in the above example would be dealt with on similar lines, and the method is applicable to all outstanding liabilities of this nature.

Dr.   MORTGAGE INTEREST   *Cr.*

			£				£
July 4	Cash . . .		150	Dec. 31	Profit and Loss A/c. . .		300
Dec. 31	Outstanding half-year's interest . . c/d		150				
			£300				£300
				Dec. 31	Balance (interest outstanding) . . b/d		150

The full £300 will then be transferred to Profit and Loss Account, and the credit balance of £150 shown as a current liability in the Balance Sheet.

Had the above example formed part of an exercise the rent and interest already paid would have appeared in the given Trial Balance, and the outstanding liabilities as a footnote to the Trial Balance somewhat as below—

TRIAL BALANCE

	Dr.	Cr.
	£	
AMONG OTHER ITEMS OF COMPLETE TRIAL BALANCE		
Rent	600	
Interest on 6% mortgage of £5,000	150	

In preparing the Trading and Profit and Loss Account and Balance Sheet the following must be taken into consideration—

(a) Provide £200 for one quarter's rent outstanding.
(b) Half-year's interest (£150) on mortgage is due but has not been paid.

The student should think out the Ledger entries required for the adjustments, though they may not be called for in the test paper. As stated above, one entry only is required for each item *in* the Trial Balance as the double-entry was made before the extraction of the Trial Balance.

The adjustment of £200 owing must be dealt with twice. First, it must be debited to the Profit and Loss Account, together with the £600 item (thereby making the £800 shown as transferred in the Rent Account on p. 119); and then it must be shown as a current liability in the Balance Sheet as the credit balance of the Rent Account.

Similarly, the interest owing and the interest paid must be debited to Profit and Loss Account, and the second entry for the interest owing will be as an outstanding liability in the Balance Sheet.

Many students are unable to make their Balance Sheets agree because they fail to deal twice with the adjustments.

Payments in Advance

Some payments, as for rent, rates, and insurance, may represent, wholly or in part, payments in advance. These will need to be apportioned so that part is properly charged against this year's profits, and the remainder is carried forward against next year's profits. Each financial period then bears the expenses of the period.

Example

In a Trial Balance extracted on 31st December appeared—

				£
Rates and Water	.	.	.	1,800
Insurance .	.	.	.	984

but of these sums the following amounts were payments in advance in respect of the succeeding year—

					£
Rates	.	.	.	.	327
Insurance .	.	.	.	232

Show the adjustments necessary in the respective accounts.

The Rates and Water Account will have a debit of £1,800 from which the item in the Trial Balance is drawn. Without due apportionment the whole of this would be transferred to the debit of Profit and Loss Account. But £1,473 (£1,800 less £327) only should be charged against this year's profits. It is necessary, therefore, to reduce the balance by £327 and carry forward that sum as a charge against next year's profits.

The method is to credit £327 to the existing Rates and Water Account, and bring down that sum as the opening balance on the new account for the next trading period.

Dr.					RATES AND WATER			Cr.
	Cash .	.	.	£ 1,800	Dec. 31	Rates in advance . Profit and Loss A/c. .	c/d	£ 327 1,473
				£1,800				£1,800
Dec. 31	Balance (Rates in advance) .	.	b/d	327				

The balance on the new account will be shown under the current assets in the Balance Sheet as "Rates Paid in Advance." Similar treatment will be given to the Insurance entries.

Dr.					INSURANCE			Cr.
	Cash . . .			£984	Dec. 31	Insurance paid in advance . . Profit and Loss A/c. . .	c/d	£ 232 752
				£984				£984
Dec. 31	Balance . .	b/d	232					

If the Ledger accounts are not required, but the final accounts are to be prepared from the given Trial Balance, the twofold effect of the adjustment must not be lost sight of. The Trial Balance item will be dealt with once only. The adjustment will be treated in the Profit and Loss Account and shown in the Balance Sheet.

The entries in the Profit and Loss Account (debit side) should be set out as below—

		£	£
Dec. 31	Rates and Water	1,800	
	Less Rates in Advance . . .	327	
			1,473
	Insurance	984	
	Less payment in advance . . .	232	
			752

and in the Balance Sheet (assets side)—

		£
Rates paid in advance . . .	327	
Insurance	232	

Other Adjustments

In practice many adjustments may have to be made to ensure that the Balance Sheet shows the correct financial position, and that the profit for the year is the true net profit for the period. Some of the more common adjustments necessary are discussed below to assist the student in understanding the principles upon which their treatment is decided. In any adjustment the effect upon the accounts should be thought out. If necessary, for the sake of clarity, the Ledger accounts should be sketched, and it is again emphasized that all adjustments affect both the Balance Sheet and either the Trading or the Profit and Loss Account, and must be entered twice in the final accounts as against once for the Trial Balance items.

Frequently the adjustments are simple variations of outstanding liabilities and payments in advance as already discussed. Examples of these and other forms of adjustments are given below with brief comments on their treatment in the preparation of final accounts from a given Trial Balance. In parenthesis a note is also made of the treatment in the Ledger accounts.

£50 commission is due to a traveller for the December quarter.

The commission owing should be brought into account by debiting it to Profit and Loss Account, and, as the traveller is a creditor for £50, it should also appear as a current liability in the Balance Sheet.

(Debit Commission Account, credit to the Traveller's Personal Account.)

Loan Interest due to J. Robinson on 31st December has not been passed through the firm's books.

The principal sum and the rate of interest will be disclosed in the exercise. The interest outstanding should be calculated and taken to the debit of Profit and Loss Account and shown as current liability in the Balance Sheet.

(Debit Interest on Loan Account and bring down a similar sum as a credit balance on the account for the new period.)

£500 of the Advertising expenditure is to be carried forward.

A firm may engage in a special advertising campaign and decide to spread the cost over a period of years instead of charging the whole cost against the current year's profits. A proportion of the cost is therefore carried to Profit and Loss

Account, and the remainder carried forward as a temporary asset which appears in the Balance Sheet. In the above case, £500 is deducted from the Trial Balance item for advertising on its being debited to Profit and Loss Account, and the £500 shown among the current assets of the Balance Sheet.

(Credit Advertising Account £500 and carry down a similar sum to the debit of the account for the new period.)

Transfer to Reserve of £10,000.

Debit Profit and Loss Account, credit Reserve Account, the balance of which will appear on the left-hand side of the Balance Sheet.

Unused office stationery, stamps, etc., are valued at 31st December at £30.

Deduct £30 from the Trial Balance item for stationery and stamps and take the net amount to the debit of Profit and Loss Account. Show £30 as a current asset in the Balance Sheet.

(Credit £30 to Stationery and Stamps Account and carry down a similar sum to the debit of the account for the new period.)

The stock of catalogues on hand at 31st December was valued at £200.

Deduct £200 from the Trial Balance item and take the net amount to the debit of Profit and Loss Account. Show £200 as a current asset in the Balance Sheet.

(Credit Catalogues Account, £200, and bring down a similar sum to the debit of the account for the new period.)

Free samples to the value of £1,500 were distributed during the year to 31st December, but no record was made in the accounts.

Debit the value of samples distributed to the Profit and Loss Account as an expense, and make a corresponding credit entry in the Trading Account.

Goods (£200) received from H. Masters were taken into stock on 31st December, but no entry was made in the Purchases Journal in respect of these until 5th January.

Care should be exercised that goods are not taken into stock before the entries have been made in the books of account.

However, in this case, the goods have been taken into stock and included in the year's end stocktaking. Therefore, Closing Stock must be reduced by £200 both in the Trading Account and the Balance Sheet. Alternatively, as some of the goods may have been sold, Purchases Account should be increased by £200 and the total of creditors increased by £200 to include the amount due to H. Masters.

The Trial Balance items for Rent and Rates, Insurance, Lighting, and Heating are to be apportioned nine-tenths to the warehouse and one-tenth to the office.

The apportionment of rent and similar items between the warehouse and office is for the purpose of separating trading and administrative expenses. The nine-tenths attributable to the warehouse should be debited to the Trading Account, and the one-tenth office proportion debited to Profit and Loss Account.

If the instructions ask for rent or other expense to be adjusted to take into account an amount in arrear or paid in advance, such adjustment should be made *before* apportionment between warehouse and office.

During the year the owner of the business took goods valued at £80 from stock for his own use. No entries had been made in the books.

Such goods are usually taken out at cost price. Credit the amount to the Purchases Account and debit Drawings Account as the value is a withdrawal in kind on account of profits. In the Ledger a personal account in the owner's name should be opened to which goods taken out should be debited. At the close of the trading period the balance of the account should be transferred to the owner's Drawings Account or, in the absence of a Drawings Account, to the debit of Capital Account.

Packing Materials

When goods are specially packed before they are ready for sale this may be regarded as an operating or trading cost and may therefore be debited to the Trading Account. However, where there is no indication that this is the case, the cost of packing should be treated as a selling expense and debited to the Profit and Loss Account.

Should a charge be made for packing, as is the practice where the materials are costly, the customer's account should be debited. On the return of the empties the account should be credited. Special columns for packing are usually added to the Sales Journal and Returns Inwards Journal, and the respective credit and debit entries, corresponding to the above entries in the customer's account, would be completed on the totals of these columns being posted to a Packing Materials Account in the Ledger.

The above are typical adjustments, but the list cannot be, and is not intended to be, exhaustive. A careful study of these, however, should enable the student to deal correctly with any normal variations in form that the adjustments may take.

EXERCISE 69

The following items are taken from a Trial Balance at 31st December—

		£
Rent	.	900
Wages	.	3,600
Commission	.	500

The following expenses were outstanding—

		£
One quarter's rent	.	300
Three days' wages to 31st December	.	35
Traveller's Commission	.	40

Give the Journal entries for the above adjustments and set out the Ledger accounts as they would appear after the adjustments have been made.

EXERCISE 70

The following are items as they appeared in a Trial Balance—

		£
Insurance	.	76
Rates	.	400
Advertising	.	2,000

The following adjustments are necessary—

		£
Insurance paid in advance	.	19
Rates paid in advance	.	100
Advertising to be carried forward	.	1,000

Give the entries to carry these adjustments into effect and show how they affect the Balance Sheet.

EXERCISE 71

A. Chapman, who carries on business as a grocer, takes goods from his
stock for his private use to the value of £52 during the year ending 31st March,
19.., but no record is made of this in his books. Show how you would adjust
his accounts at the end of the year in order to show the correct position.

(R.S.A.)

EXERCISE 72

B. Temperley's financial position on 1st March, 19.., was as follows—

	£
Cash in hand	40·85
Debtor: B. Wilkins	82·00
Plant and Machinery	1,600·00
Fixtures and Fittings	780·00
Stock	586·00
Overdraft	280·00
Creditor: J. Jephson	8·85

Open, through the Journal Proper, the accounts necessary to record the
above in Temperley's Ledgers, and post thereto, using the proper subsidiary
books, the following transactions—

Mar. 2. Paid rent by cheque, £40.
    5. Sold goods on credit to W. Jacques, £25.
       Sold goods on credit to S. Manners, £380.
    8. Received £50 on account from B. Wilkins, by cheque.
   11. Bought goods on credit from R. Stokes, Ltd., £210.
   13. Paid wages in cash £36. Cashed a cheque for office cash, £30.
   16. Sold goods to R. Black, £290. Received a cheque.
   19. Drew from cash for private purposes, £15.
   23. Bought goods on credit from J. Jephson, £160, less 10 per cent
       trade discount.
   28. Learned that B. Wilkins was declared bankrupt. Wrote his balance
       off as a bad debt.
   30. Received payment by cheque from W. Jacques less 2½ per cent
       cash discount.
       Paid rates by cheque, £60.
   31. Sold goods on credit to M. Newson, £80.
       Sold goods on credit to S. Steele, £40.
       Paid carriage on above deliveries by cheque, £9.

Extract Trial Balance (Totals, £4,032·47.)
Prepare a Trading and Profit and Loss Account and a Balance Sheet, after
taking into consideration the following—

(*a*) The stock on hand at the end of the month was valued at £520.
(*b*) Wages unpaid at the end of the month amounted to £22.
(*c*) The whole of the amount paid for rates refers to the next accounting
    period.
(*d*) A provision of 5 per cent on the sundry debtors is to be created for
    possible bad debts.

(e) Plant and machinery is to be depreciated at 10 per cent and fixtures and fittings at 5 per cent.

(Gross Profit, £395. Net Profit, £31·37. Balance Sheet totals, £3,255·85.)

EXERCISE 73

The figures of the following Trial Balance were extracted from the books of W. Walker, a wholesale provision merchant, on 31st December, 19.. —

	£	£
Capital		17,874
Lease (to run 10 years from 1st January)	5,000	
Advertising	127	
Motor vans	927	
Purchases	68,485	
Postage	138	
Lighting and Heating	91	
Wages	2,837	
Rates and Water	101	
Telephone	34	
Furniture and Fittings	1,104	
Sales		73,498
Returns Inwards and Outwards	56	392
Bad debts	26	
Insurance	192	
Debtors	4,882	
Creditors		8,405
Cash in hand	352	
Balance with Bank	3,792	
Stock at 1st January	12,025	
	£100,169	£100,169

Prepare Trading and Profit and Loss Accounts for the year ended 31st December, and Balance Sheet at that date. In preparing the accounts the following matters should be taken into consideration—

(a) The stock at 31st December was valued at £10,787.

(b) An appropriate amount of depreciation should be written off the lease.

(c) 20 per cent per annum on cost (£1,250) should be written off motor vans.

(d) One-third of the insurance refers to next year.

(e) Make a bad debt provision of £300.

(f) 10 per cent per annum should be written off furniture and fittings.

Indicate in the accounts the rate of gross profit earned on the sales.

(N.B. The student can presume that all Ledger entries other than for the Trading and Profit and Loss Account have been made.)

ADDITIONAL EXERCISES

Graded Book-keeping Exercises, Nos. 96 to 106.

CHAPTER XXI

GOODWILL

The term "goodwill" is often seen in Press advertisements for the sale of businesses. The owner is anxious to sell and offers premises, fittings, and stock for a certain sum of money, and adds, for example, "Goodwill, £2,000." The owner may have started the business, and he considers that the prospect of customers continuing to purchase at the shop is worth £2,000 to the prospective buyer. Such a consideration is termed the goodwill. A new concern has no goodwill. It has to be created. It may arise from the location of the business (e.g. a tobacconist near a railway station), or from a reputation for value and service. However the business has grown, a new owner steps into it ready made, and with similar service he may at least expect the greater proportion of custom to continue.

The value of the goodwill varies from business to business as conditions cannot be equal even in concerns in the same trade. Again, the prospect of custom continuing under new ownership is greater where the location is the chief reason, than in a case where custom has been attracted by the personal skill of the owner. The value of the goodwill is in the expectation of good profits from the continued custom, and such value is based on the assumption that the profits of the business will continue to be above those which could be earned by anybody starting a new business. If in a particular trade a new business could earn £400 a year, then an established business earning, on an average, £1,000 a year would be earning £600 a year above the normal for that type of business. Goodwill would be based on this figure and calculated at three to five times this super profit, as the £600 would be called.

In arriving at the figure of average profits it is important to take several years into account and also to note whether the trend of those profits is increasing or decreasing.

Goodwill in Accounts

As an example let it be assumed that Smith buys Brown's business for an all-in sum of £10,000 made up as follows—

	£
Freehold Premises	2,500
Furniture and Fittings	500
Book Debts	600
Stock	4,400
Goodwill	2,000

The capital cost to Smith is £10,000. The usual assets total £8,000, but he has acquired something of value, goodwill, for £2,000. This also is an asset for which in turn, if he sells the business, he may be able to obtain cash. Smith then must open a Ledger account to record this asset, and must also show it as an asset in the Balance Sheet of the business as a set-off against the capital of £10,000.

Dr.		GOODWILL			Cr.
	Cash	£ 2,000			£

Smith's Balance Sheet, if prepared directly after the purchase, would appear as below—

BALANCE SHEET

	£		£	£
Capital	10,000	Goodwill		2,000
		Fixed Assets—		
		Freehold Premises	2,500	
		Furniture and Fittings	500	
				3,000
		Current Assets—		
		Debtors	600	
		Stock	4,400	
				5,000
	£10,000			£10,000

Goodwill can be considered as the *total value of the business* less the *value of all the fixed assets and current assets* (such as premises and stock). It is always difficult to value exactly and, because it has no substance (i.e. it is not "real" in the sense that premises and motor vehicles are "real"), it is described as an *Intangible Asset*.

Writing Down Goodwill

Though the goodwill appears in the Balance Sheet at cost it necessarily fluctuates in value as profits rise or fall from year to year, and as other conditions affecting custom influence the business. Of course, the business might reach such low water that it would be unsaleable as a going concern and the asset would then be actually worthless, though still appearing in the Balance Sheet. It is not wise or possible to attempt to change the Balance Sheet figure according to these fluctuations from time to time, but it may be wise financial policy to lessen the value, especially if the business does not show increasing profits.

At the end of a financial year Smith above might decide to reduce the value of goodwill by £1,000. The entries necessary to record this decision are—

Credit Goodwill Account.
Debit Profit and Loss Account.

JOURNAL

	£	£
Profit and Loss Account	1,000	
Goodwill		1,000
Goodwill written off.		

The balance standing on Goodwill Account will then be £1,000, and this will be the value of goodwill in the Balance Sheet. The profit available for division will be lessened by the £1,000 written off. If, however, the business is sound, the writing down of the goodwill by £1,000 has created a hidden reserve of that amount. In other words, this asset is worth more at the moment than the value placed upon it in the Balance Sheet.

Should the writing down of the goodwill appear in an exercise as an adjustment to be made in preparing final accounts from the given Trial Balance, the item must be dealt with twice as it has not gone through the books. Debit Profit and Loss Account with the amount proposed to be written off, and show the goodwill in the Balance Sheet at the Trial Balance figure less the amount written off.

In practice Goodwill Account is seldom found in the books of sole traders but is commonly included in the books of partnerships. Accounts of partners are considered in the next two chapters, but it may be useful to note here that adjustments to the Goodwill Account of partnerships are made through the Appropriation Account.

CHAPTER XXII

PARTNERSHIPS (I): PARTNERSHIP ACCOUNTS AND THE PROFIT AND LOSS ACCOUNT

Two or more persons carrying on business together with a view of making a profit constitute a partnership. Hitherto we have been concerned with the accounts of the sole trader—the sole owner of the business who alone provides the capital and takes all the profits and bears all the losses attaching to his venture. But many businesses are owned by more than one person, and certain additional accounts are necessary in order that financial relations of the partners with the business may be adequately recorded.

Partnerships must, of course, have at least two members and twenty is the upper limit legally permitted. The persons who have agreed to trade together are called collectively the firm. It is obvious that from the outset they must have some understanding between them on certain points, e.g. how much capital each shall put into the business, how they shall divide the profits. To prevent differences arising in the future an agreement is usually drawn up and signed by the partners. This agreement is called the Partnership Deed or the Articles of Partnership, and contains such terms as the following—

(a) The period the partnership is to last.
(b) The amount of capital each partner is to contribute.
(c) How profits and losses are to be shared.
(d) The amounts each partner may draw out of the business.
(e) The rate of interest to be allowed on capital, if at all.
(f) The salaries, if any, to which the partners are entitled.
(g) That proper accounts are to be kept and audited.

Partnerships are governed by the Partnership Act, 1890, and in the absence of a partnership agreement, whether in writing or not, certain rules contained in Section 24 of that Act apply, e.g.—

1. Profits must be divided equally and the partners must contribute equally to the losses which may arise.

2. No partner is entitled to interest on capital.

3. No partner is entitled to a salary or remuneration for acting in the partnership business.

4. Loans or advances by a partner to the firm are to bear interest at 5 per cent per annum.

5. That the partnership books are to be kept at the principal place of business and that every partner has access to them and may copy any of them.

It is essential, therefore, for the book-keeper to a partnership firm to know the provisions of the partnership agreement, if any, and the rules which apply if there is no agreement. Those of the partners who take an active part in the business are known as the *active* or working partners. A partner may, however, cease to take an active part in the conduct of the firm's business though retaining an interest in the partnership. He is known as a Sleeping or Dormant partner.

Limited partners are allowed by the Limited Partnerships Act, 1907, but there must be one or more general partners in the firm. The limited partner is allowed to put capital into the business and yet must not take any active part in its management, though sharing the profits. His liability for the debts of the firm is limited (hence his name) to the amount of capital he contributes. The general partners, whether active or dormant, are, like the sole trader, answerable for the debts of the business, even to the extent of their private fortunes.

Partnership Accounts

Whether the business is owned by partners or a sole trader, no difference is occasioned in the record of the business transactions. The Purchases and Sales, Cash Book, and Ledger accounts for customers and suppliers remain the same. The sole difference is in the record of ownership of the capital and the division of profits with such other special accounts, as for interest on capital, as the terms of the partnership demand.

Capital Accounts. Separate capital accounts must be kept for each partner in which the amount paid into the business by him is recorded.

Partners' Drawings. In the accounts of the sole trader the net profit is credited and his drawings debited to his Capital Account. The partners' Capital Accounts may be kept similarly, but it is usual to provide that the capital be fixed, and that whatever is due to or by the partner as the result of the year's work by recorded as a debt due by or to the firm separate from the capital. Under this arrangement the Capital Account rests unaltered until such time, if at all, as there is an alteration in the partner's capital. The profits to which the partners are entitled and the sums they have drawn out on account of profit are recorded in separate accounts called Drawings (or Current Accounts. If the partner's Capital Account and Drawings (or Current) Account were combined in one account only, we should have in it the information usually contained in the Capital Account of a sole trader.

Example

A. Beaumont and J. Hamel are in partnership under the firm name of Beaumont, Hamel & Co. Beaumont contributed £2,000 and Hamel £1,000 capital in cash as on 1st January. Profits are to be divided equally. Beaumont may draw £150 and Hamel £100 quarterly on 31st March, 30th June, 30th September, and 31st December. The profits for the year 19.. amounted to £1,750.

The transactions that resulted in a net profit of £1,750 for the year would be recorded in the firm's books in a form no different from that of a sole trader. The only additional record required, because of there being two joint owners, is as follows—

1. Separate Capital Accounts for each partner.

Dr.				A. BEAUMONT'S CAPITAL ACCOUNT			Cr.
			£	19.. Jan. 1	Bank . . .	CB	£ 2,000

Dr.				J. HAMEL'S CAPITAL ACCOUNT			Cr.
			£	19.. Jan. 1	Bank . . .	CB	£ 1,000

2. Separate Current or Drawings Accounts for each partner. The balances of these accounts appear in the Balance Sheet either as assets or liabilities, according to whether the balances are amounts due by the firm to the partners, or vice versa.

Dr.					A. BEAUMONT'S CURRENT ACCOUNT		Cr.
19.. Mar. 31 June 30 Sept. 30 Dec. 31	Bank . . . Bank . . . Bank . . . Bank . . .	CB CB CB CB	£ 150 150 150 150	19.. Dec. 31	Share of Profits (*Note*. The Debit entry for this item is in the Profit and Loss Appropriation A/c.)		£ 875

Dr.					J. HAMEL'S CURRENT ACCOUNT		Cr.
19.. Mar. 31 June 30 Sept. 30 Dec. 31	Bank . . . Bank . . . Bank . . . Bank . . .	CB CB CB CB	£ 100 100 100 100	19.. Dec. 31	Share of Profits (*Note*. The Debit entry for this item is in the Profit and Loss Appropriation A/c.)		£ 875

The Cash Book would contain the following entries among the ordinary receipts and payments. (Bank columns only are shown.)

Dr.			CASH BOOK				Cr.
			Bank				Bank
19.. Jan. 1	A. Beaumont L. Hamel	.	£ 2,000 1,000	19.. Mar. 31 June 30 Sept. 30 Dec. 31	A. Beaumont J. Hamel A. Beaumont J. Hamel A. Beaumont J. Hamel A. Beaumont J. Hamel	. . . .	£ 150 100 150 100 150 100 150 100

The Profit and Loss Account

It is now the usual practice to divide the Profit and Loss Account of a partnership business into two sections. The first contains the usual entries of the trading concern. The net profit is then carried down to the second section and there divided between the partners in the agreed proportions, the double-entry being made by crediting their respective Current Accounts. If the year's trading results in a net loss, the amount would be carried down to the debit of the second section, and the division of the loss between the partners would be placed on the credit side, and the double-entry for the division made by debiting the partners' Current Account with the appropriate proportions of the loss. This second section is called the Appropriation Account.

The advantage of the second section is that it gives at a glance the total profit or loss that is to be divided between the partners.

PROFIT AND LOSS ACCOUNT (Appropriation Section only)

	£				£
Share of Profit— A. Beaumont . J. Hamel. .	875 875		Trading Profit .	b/d	1,750
	£1,750				£1,750

EXERCISE 74

On 1st July, 19.., T. Raven and M. Moore enter into partnership and commence to trade under the firm name of Raven & Moore. Raven contributed £500 and Moore £300 as capital, which was paid direct into the firm's banking account. They agreed to share profits equally.

During the month Raven drew £60 and Moore £50 on account of profits. The net trading profit for the month was £290. Show the Appropriation Account, the Partners' Capital and Current Accounts, and the appropriate entries in the firm's Balance Sheet.

ADDITIONAL EXERCISES

Graded Book-keeping Exercises, Nos. 107 to 109.

CHAPTER XXIII

PARTNERSHIPS (II): INTEREST ON CAPITAL, PARTNERSHIP SALARIES, INTEREST ON DRAWINGS, AND THE BALANCE SHEET

IN the example in the preceding chapter Beaumont and Hamel share profits equally but have unequal capitals. It may have been agreed to divide profits equally as each gives all his energy and time to the business. Beaumont might, however, claim that part of the profit results from the extra capital he has introduced, viz. £2,000 as against Hamel's £1,000. The profits, for example, of a printing firm depend largely on the number of machines in use.

Interest on Capital

To give some compensation in these and similar cases, it is usual to provide in the Partnership Agreement that the partners shall receive interest on their capital at an agreed percentage. This is usually about 5 per cent per annum, somewhere near the return on money invested in good securities, and is calculated on the partners' capital as it stands at the beginning of the trading period.

The amounts to be given to the partners as interest must be charged, of course, against the profits of the business, leaving less to divide between them. The combined total of interest and profit going to each partner will differ from the former equal division of profit, and will be in favour of the partner introducing the larger capital.

The entries in the books are—

Debit Appropriation Account.

Credit the amounts to the partners' respective Current Accounts.

139

Partnership Salaries

One partner may give more time to the business than another, or a former manager may be taken into partnership but have little or no capital in the concern, and, consequently, little to come in the form of profits. For these and similar reasons the partnership agreement may provide that the partner shall receive a salary.

The arrangement to pay the salary may take one of two forms. The partner may be *paid* the salary during the trading period, or it may be agreed to place the amount to his credit at the close of the trading period. In either case the sum is debited to a Partnership Salaries Account for transfer eventually to the Profit and Loss Appropriation Account. If the salary has been paid the credit entry is in the Cash Book. Where it is not paid but is to be credited to the partner, it is placed to the credit of his Current Account along with the other items, e.g. share of profits and interest on capital, to which he is entitled and may draw upon in the future.

Interest on Drawings

Partners' drawings are sums withdrawn from the business in anticipation of the profits to which the partners expect they will be entitled at the close of the financial year. Sometimes the drawings are made at regular intervals and in the same ratio as the partners have agreed to share profits and losses. In other cases sums are withdrawn at irregular intervals and in varying amounts. Under the former method no one partner has a financial advantage over the others, but, in the latter case, the arrangement may work out that partners are withdrawing cash on account of profits more frequently or in larger amounts than other partners, and, consequently, do receive a monetary advantage. If left in the business, such sums might bring in further profit or interest. Partners who make heavy drawings in anticipation of profit are thus depriving the business of working capital. Those whose drawings are smaller help the business by their restraint. To compensate for these inequalities, partnership agreements often provide that interest is to be charged on drawings. The rate of interest is usually 5 per cent per annum calculated from the date of withdrawal until the end of the accounting period.

The entries required in the books are—

Credit Profit and Loss Appropriation Account.
Debit the partners' respective Current Accounts.

The interest charged to the individual partners is a gain to the firm.

In order to ascertain easily the total interest to be charged against the partner, the current accounts may have additional columns for memorandum purposes so that the interest may be noted at the time of each withdrawal. At the close of the year the total of the interest column is transferred to the true debit column and the Current Account, and the same sum credited to the Profit and Loss Appropriation Account. These columns and the entries for interest on capital and partners' salaries are shown in the following example.

Example

A. Beaumont and J. Hamel are in partnership under the firm name of Beaumont, Hamel & Co., contributing capital in cash on 1st January £2,000 and £1,000 respectively. The partnership deed provides that interest be allowed on capital and charged on drawings at 5 per cent per annum, that profits are to be divided equally, that Beaumont may withdraw £150 and Hamel £100 on 31st March, 30th June, 30th September, and 31st December, and that Hamel is to have a salary of £200 per annum, £100 of which is to be paid on 30th June, and the remaining £100 is to be credited to his account. Net trading profit for year 19.. amounted to £1,750.

Dr.				A. BEAUMONT'S CAPITAL ACCOUNT		Cr.
			£	19.. Jan. 1	Bank . . .	£ 2,000

Dr.				J. HAMEL'S CAPITAL ACCOUNT		Cr.
			£	19.. Jan. 1	Bank . . .	£ 1,000

Dr.   CASH BOOK (Bank Columns only)   *Cr.*

			Bank				Bank
19..			£	19..			£
Jan. 1	A. Beaumont	.	2,000	Mar. 31	A. Beaumont	.	150
	J. Hamel	.	1,000		J. Hamel .		100
				June 30	A. Beaumont	.	150
					J. Hamel .	.	100
					J. Hamel (Salary)	.	100
				Sept. 30	A. Beaumont	.	150
					J. Hamel .	.	100
				Dec. 31	A. Beaumont	.	150
					J. Hamel .	.	100

Dr.   PARTNERSHIP SALARIES ACCOUNT   *Cr.*

			£				£
19..				19..			
June 30	Bank .	.	100	Dec. 31	Appropriation		200
Dec. 31	J. Hamel's				A/c. .	.	
	Current A/c.	.	100				
			£200				£200

A. Beaumont's Current Account

Dr.

		Months	Interest	Drawings				Cr.
19..			£	£	19..			£
Mar. 31	Bank .	9	5·62	150·00	Dec. 31	Interest on Capital . .		100·00
June 30	Bank .	6	3·75	150·00		Share of Profits . .		709·37
Sept. 30	Bank .	3	1·87	150·00				
Dec. 31	Bank .			150·00				
	Interest		11·24	11·24				
	Balance . . . . c/d			198·13				
				£809·37				£809·37
					19..			
					Jan. 1	Balance .	b/d	198·13

J. Hamel's Current Account

Dr.

		Months	Interest	Drawings				Cr.
19..			£	£	19..			£
Mar. 31	Bank .	9	3·75	100·00	Dec. 1	Interest on Capital . .		50·00
June 30	Bank .	6	2·50	100·00		Salary . .		100·00
Sept. 30	Bank .	3	1·25	100·00		Share of Profits . .		709·37
Dec. 31	Bank .			100·00				
	Interest		7·50	7·50				
	Balance . . . . c/d			451·87				
				£859·37				£859·37
					19..			
					Jan. 1	Balance .	b/d	451·87

Dr.		PROFIT AND LOSS APPROPRIATION ACCOUNT			Cr.
	£		Trading Profit .		£ 1,750·00

Interest on
    Capital   .
	150·00		Interest on
			    Drawings .
					18·74

Partnership Salary .	200·00				
Share of Profit: A. Beaumont . J. Hamel .	709·37 709·37				
	£1,768·74				£1,768·74

The Balance Sheet

Where the partners have separate Capital and Current Accounts, it is usual to set out the details of the Current Accounts in the Balance Sheet for information purposes. The liabilities side of the Balance Sheet of the above firm will therefore appear as below. The items are confined to the ownership accounts, the trading items being omitted.

BALANCE SHEET (LIABILITIES SIDE ONLY)

AS AT 31ST DECEMBER, 19..

	£	£	£
CAPITAL—			
A. Beaumont		2,000·00	
J. Hamel		1,000·00	
			3,000·00
CURRENT ACCOUNTS—			
A. Beaumont—			
Share of Profits . . .	709·37		
Interest on Capital . .	100·00		
		809·37	
Less Drawings . . .	600·00		
Interest thereon . .	11·24		
		611·24	
			198·13
J. Hamel—			
Share of Profits . . .	709·37		
Interest on Capital . .	50·00		
Salary	100·00		
		859·37	
Less Drawings . . .	400·00		
Interest thereon . .	7·50		
		407·50	
			451·87

EXERCISE 75

T. Margate and F. Westgate commence business in partnership on 1st December, 19... T. Margate pays £1,000 and F. Westgate £500 into the firm's banking account as their respective capitals. They agree—

(a) That profits and losses shall be divided, two-thirds to Margate and one-third to Westgate.

(b) That Westgate shall be paid £20 monthly as partnership salary.

(c) No interest shall be charged on drawings, but shall be allowed on capital at 5 per cent per annum.

Record the above payments in of capital and proceed to enter the following transactions in the partnership books—

		£
Dec.	2. Withdrew cash from bank for office purposes	100·00
	4. Bought goods for cheque	600·00
	6. Bought from T. Tidy & Sons, goods	400·00
	9. Sold to H. Higgins, goods	276·50
	15. Paid sundry expenses in cash	5·25
	19. Bought office furniture for cash	25·00
	20. H. Higgins paid on account by cheque	100·00
	23. Sold goods for cash	156·00
	Paid cash into bank	150·00
	24. Sold to L. Smart, goods	84·00
	Partners' drawings by cheque: T. Margate	40·00
	F. Westgate	30·00
	30. Partnership salary paid to F. Westgate by cheque	20·00

Take out Trial Balance.

(Cash Balance, £75·75. Bank Balance, £960. Trial Balance totals, £2,416·50.)

Prepare Trading and Profit and Loss Accounts as at 31st December and Balance Sheet as at that date. Stock on hand, £670. Interest on capital, £4·16 and £2·09 respectively.

(Gross Profit, £186·50. Net Trading Profit, £181·25. Balance Sheet totals, £1,991·25.)

EXERCISE 76

Jones, Brown, and Robinson are in partnership and their partnership agreement contains the following provisions—

1. That the partners' fixed capitals shall be: Jones, £10,000; Brown, £6,000; and Robinson, £4,000.

2. That Jones and Brown are each to be credited with a salary of £500 per year.

3. Interest to be allowed on capital at 5 per cent per annum.

4. That profits and losses are to be shared: Jones, one-half; Brown, three-tenths; and Robinson, one-fifth.

5. No interest to be charged on drawings.

During the year 19.. the partners' drawings were: Jones, £1,000; Brown, £800; and Robinson, £600. The Profit and Loss Account for that year showed a trading profit of £3,500 before taking into consideration the interest on capital or partners' salaries.

Show the Capital and Current Accounts of the partners as at the close of the year.

EXERCISE 77

From the following Trial Balance you are required to prepare Trading and Profit and Loss Accounts for the year ended 31st January, 19.., and a Balance Sheet as on that date—

TRIAL BALANCE, 31st January, 19..

	Dr.	Cr.
	£	£
Capital: L. Smith		2,000·00
G. Dickson		1,000·00
Bank Overdraft		1,000·00
Sales and Sales Returns	140·40	3,475·05
Sundry Creditors		496·20
Purchases	2,980·30	
Sundry Debtors	503·50	
Stock	560·15	
Trade Expenses	471·15	
Partner's (G. Dickson) Salary	200·00	
Bank Charges	15·75	
Plant and Machinery	3,000·00	
Additions to ditto during the Year	100·00	
	£7,971·25	£7,971·25

The stock on 31st January, 19.., was valued at £1,465·00. The partners share profits equally.

(Gross Profit, £788·05.   Net Trading Profit, £772·30.   Balance Sheet
totals, £5.068·50.)   (R.S.A.)

EXERCISE 78

S. Holmes and B. Watson are in partnership, contributing in cash, Holmes £2,000, Watson £1,000. They agree (1) to divide profits and losses equally; (2) that interest shall be allowed on capital and charged on drawings at 5 per cent per annum; and (3) that Watson shall receive a salary of £500 per annum to be credited half-yearly to his account—

		£
Jan.	1. Current Account opened and cash paid in	3,000
	24. Paid Advertising Account by cheque	50
	27. Drew from bank for office cash	40
Feb.	10. Bought job line of goods and paid by cheque	1,500
Mar.	3. Sold to J. Whiteside, goods	1,200
	25. Sold for cheque, goods	1,250
	31. Partners' drawings by cheque—	
	Holmes	300
	Watson	200
Apr.	17. Purchased job stock of goods for cheque	1,750
	26. Paid transport expenses in cash	10
May	24. Sold goods and received cheque	2,000
June	30. Paid warehouse rent in cash	25
	Partners' drawings—	
	Holmes	300
	Watson	200

Take out Trial Balance.

(Trial Balance totals, £7,450.)

Prepare final accounts for the half-year ending 30th June. Stock on hand, £1,000.

(Gross Profit, £2,200. Net Profit for division, £1,796·25. Balance Sheet totals, £4,115.)

ADDITIONAL EXERCISES

Graded Book-keeping Exercises, Nos. 110 to 125.

CHAPTER XXIV

USES OF THE JOURNAL PROPER:
CORRECTION OF ERRORS

THE functions of the Journal were explained in Chapter IX and rules were given for deciding whether Journal entries were necessary.

Having determined that a Journal entry is required, the student has then to decide in which of the five Journals, with which he is now familiar, the entry must be made. This should present no difficulty since any entry which cannot be classified as Purchases, Sales, Returns Inwards or Returns Outwards must be made in the Journal Proper, unless it records a routine cash transaction.

The entries made in the Journal Proper can be conveniently grouped thus —

(*a*) Opening entries (which the student is little likely to meet with other than in exercises or examinations).

(*b*) The transfers between Ledger accounts, especially those necessary when preparing the final accounts.

(*c*) Purchases of fixed assets.

(*d*) Sales of fixed assets.

(*e*) The creation, increase or decrease of reserves and provisions.

(*f*) Correction or errors found in the books.

(*g*) Any special entry which cannot be dealt with through any of the other Journals.

The last of these categories includes a great variety of entries, some of which would require several debits to a credit or vice versa, as with the opening entries.

Example

S. Dyer, a customer, owes £174. His creditor accepted a cheque for £70, goods valued at £65, and a filing cabinet valued at £10 in full settlement, as Dyer is retiring from business.

The Journal entry would appear as follows—

JOURNAL

19.. Feb. 5		£	£
	Bank Account	70	
	Purchases Account	65	
	Office Equipment Account . . .	10	
	Bad Debts Account	29	
	S. Dyer		174
	Sundry assets received in part payment		
	of debt; the balance written off.		

The other category which requires explanation is (*f*) correction of errors. It should be clearly understood that rubbing out is wrong under all circumstances. Errors may be crossed out and the correction may be written neatly above, but it is better to correct errors by means of an entry through the Journal Proper and so into the Ledgers.

There are two classes of error: (1) those requiring a double-entry to correct them, and (2) those requiring either a debit or a credit entry to correct them. The first do not show up when the Trial Balance is extracted (see Chapter IV); the second group do.

Wherever possible a twofold entry should be made that will cancel out the incorrect item and at the same time ensure the correct item is posted. By way of example, consider the following Ledger accounts—

37

Dr.					P. JOHNSON			*Cr.*
19.. Jan. 9	Sales . . .	SB	£ 240	19.. Feb. 3	Bank . . .	CB	£ 100	

49

Dr.				B. Johnstone			Cr.
19.. Jan. 17	Sales . . .	SB	£ 180				£

From these it appears that P. Johnson had paid £100 on account of amount due from him. In point of fact, B. Johnstone paid the £100, but it was wrongly posted to the credit of Johnson. Now if we debit £100 to P. Johnson and credit a like sum to B. Johnstone, we shall have cancelled the original wrong entry in Johnson's account and have posted the item to the correct account. The original error is still visible, but it is better to have this frank acknowledgement of a mistake rather than to attempt to hide it by erasure or scratching out.

The entries in the books would now appear as shown below.

JOURNAL PROPER

19.. Feb. 11	P. Johnson . . . . . . B. Johnstone . . . . Correction of error—P. Johnson wrongly credited.	37 49	£ 100	£ 100

37

Dr.					P. Johnson			Cr.
19.. Jan. 9 Feb. 11	Goods . Correction of Error in Posting .	SB J	£ 240 100	19.. Feb. 3	Bank . .	CB	£ 100

49

Dr.					B. Johnstone			Cr.
19.. Jan. 17	Goods .	SB	£ 180	19.. Feb. 1	Bank . .	J	£ 100

It is not possible to correct every error by means of a double-entry. An error in casting can be corrected by crossing through the wrong figure and writing the correct figure above it. As another example, if the Purchases Book for a period had been undercast by, say, £100, and the wrong total posted to the Purchases Account, the Purchases Book total should be altered and a further item for £100 entered to the debit of the Purchases Account to make up for the undercast. Had it been an overcast, the excess would be carried to the credit of the Purchases Account. But in neither case is there a complete double-entry.

It is the practice in some business houses, if a Trial Balance disagrees, to debit or credit the amount of difference to a Suspense Account as "difference in books," thus causing a superficial agreement of the Trial Balance. For example, the credit side of a Trial Balance is £100 larger than the debit. A Suspense Account would therefore be opened and debited with the £100. Later, in searching for the error, it is discovered that the Bought Journal has been under-added by £100. The procedure will be then to debit the Purchases Account and credit the Suspense Account. If the latter account is not kept, then only the debit in the Purchases Account will be necessary. The Suspense Account will cancel out when all errors which affect the Trial Balance have been found.

Example

The Trial Balance totals of Jones & Thompson were: debit column, £80,942: credit column, £80,879. The difference was placed to Suspense Account, and after the following errors were found and corrected the Trial Balance agreed.

(i) The Returns Outwards Journal was over-added by £21.

(ii) J. Smith, a customer, was debited with £66. This was misread from the Sales Journal. He should have been debited with £6·30.

(iii) When S. Jones, a supplier, was paid his account, £24·30 cash discount was deducted. This was correctly entered in his account but was omitted from the discount column in the Cash Book.

The Journal entries and the Suspense Account would appear as follows—

JOURNAL PROPER

19..			£	£
Dec. 31	Returns Outwards Account . . . Suspense Account . . . Correction of error—Returns Outwards Journal overcast.		21·00	21·00
31	Suspense Account . . . . J. Smith . . . . . Correction of error—£6·30 in Sales Journal misread as £66 when entering in Ledger.		59·70	59·70
31	Suspense Account . . . . Discount Received Account . Correction of error—discount received from S. Jones omitted from Cash Book.		24·30	24·30

GENERAL LEDGER

SUSPENSE ACCOUNT

19..			£	19..			£

Dec. 31	J. Smith . .
	 Discount
	   Received . .
		JP
		
		 JP
			59·70
			
			 24·30
				Dec. 31	Difference in
					   books .
					 Returns .
						
						 JP
							63·00
							 21·00

			£84·00				£84·00

The student will find it useful, when dealing with correction of errors, to ask himself the following questions—

   (a) What has been done in the books?

   (b) What ought to have been done in the books?

   (c) What must I do to put the matter right?

EXERCISE 79

A book-keeper made the following errors—

19..

Jan. 3. £15 received from W. Green was posted to the credit of W. Greenhill's account in the Ledger.

     10. £40 paid for new desk was posted to Office Expenses Account.

What entries should you make in order to correct these errors? (R.S.A.)

EXERCISE 80

Show the entries required to correct the following errors—

19..

Mar. 8. New office chair, £6·50, was posted to the Sundry Expenses Account.

    19. £20 paid to G. Cooper was posted to G. Hooper's Account.

        £40 goods sold on credit to G. Evans were posted in error to E. Jevons' Account in the Ledger.

EXERCISE 81

Give the appropriate entries to rectify the following—

19..

May 10. £50 sales to W. Smith & Sons were entered in the Purchases Book and posted in error to the credit of W. Smith & Sons.

June 13. £45 cash received from J. Brown & Co. in payment of their account was credited wrongly to J. Brown's Account.

    20. £5 spent on office stationery has been debited to the Purchases Account.

    21. A new office desk, bought for cash £15, was debited to the Purchases Account.

ADDITIONAL EXERCISES

Graded Book-keeping Exercises, Nos. 126 to 136.

CHAPTER XXV

ANALYTICAL OR COLUMNAR JOURNALS

SUPPOSE a retail business has twenty departments: Glassware, Cutlery, Cosmetics, etc.; and suppose it made a profit of £20,000 during a certain period. This would give an *average* of £1,000 profit for each department for that period. But if the business made no effort to discover what was the *actual* profit made by each department, it would be running most inefficiently and probably losing money. For instance, if one department had in fact made a profit of £5,000 and another a loss of £3,000, then between them they have made £2,000 profit—an average of £1,000 profit, the same as the other departments. It is, therefore, impossible to reward suitably either the good or the bad manager.

Here is clearly a case for extracting separate Trading Accounts, and if possible Profit and Loss Accounts, for each department.

Similarly, a business selling a limited range of goods will probably need to extract separate trading figures for each of the lines sold. For example, the coal merchant will perhaps want to know the profits made on coal, coke, anthracite and any patent solid fuels he sells so that he can discard unprofitable lines or put up his prices.

To obtain separate trading figures for each department or each line of goods it will be necessary to keep separate records of stock, separate records of purchases, sales, and returns inwards and returns outwards, as well as separate figures for other expenses, such as carriage inwards, directly chargeable to Trading Account.

This information can most simply and readily be obtained by using analysis columns in the subsidiary books whereby a continuous analysis is made as the original entries are recorded.

The following two examples of analysed or columnar Sales Journals will illustrate how all four Journals can be ruled.

SALES JOURNAL

Date	Particulars	Fol.	Invoice Total	Dept. A	Dept. B	Dept. C
19..			£	£	£	£
Feb. 3	Excel, Ltd.		19·21		19·21	
7	Bright Bros. + . . .		51·42	51·42		
10	Green and Great, Ltd. .		82·32	82·32		
11	Timson, Carter, Ltd. . .		3·45			3·45

SALES JOURNAL

Date	Particulars	Fol.	Invoice Total	Suits	Over-coats	Sports-wear
19..			£	£	£	£
June 4	H. T. Jones		64·75		64·75	
8	S. Willis & Co. . . .		18·50			18·50
10	Readiwear, Ltd. . . .		211·00	108·00	76·00	27·00

It is not usual to show details of invoices in analysed Journals: if such information is required, the invoice files can be looked up. Sometimes a column for Invoice Number is added to make the searching of the files easier. Trade discount, if any, will be deducted before entries are made in analysed Journals.

At the end of each month, or other suitable period, all columns are totalled. The total of all the analysis columns will agree with the Invoice Total column. Of course, each individual invoice will be debited to the customer's account in the Sales Ledger as soon as possible after the entry is made in the Sales Journal, but instead of crediting a Sales Account, several Sales Accounts will be opened, one for each department or line of goods. Alternatively, one analysed Sales Account could be used, with separate columns for each department or line of goods. If there are large numbers of departments or lines, analyses of Ledger accounts would be rather cumbersome and separate accounts would be preferable.

The Ledger account which will certainly be analysed is the Trading and Profit and Loss Account.

EXERCISE 82

Rule a suitable Purchases Journal for Chas. Smith & Sons, who have three departments, viz. Cutlery, Tools and Gardening Implements, and Sundries, and enter therein the following transactions—

Apr. 1. Bought from Sheffield Cutlery Co., Ltd.—
          6 doz. table knives, stainless steel, mirror finish, at £1·15 a doz.
          6 pairs of grass edging cutters at £0·75 each.

      5. Bought from Long & Co., hardware merchants—
          3 "Rainmist" lawn sprinklers at £1·30 each.
          1 doz. pairs of scissors at £0·60 per pair.

      7. Bought from Blades & Smith, Ltd.—
          1 doz. razors in cases at £0·35 each.

      9. Bought from Star Manufacturing Co.—
          18 claw hammers at £0·15 each.

EXERCISE 83

D. W. Watson divides his business into two departments, viz., (1) Umbrellas and Sundries and (2) Leather Goods. Prepare a suitable Purchases Journal and record in it the following transactions—

Jan. 10. Bought from Reynard & Co.—
          3 doz. ladies' umbrellas, silk covers, assorted shades, at £1·45 each.

     15. Bought from Jardin & Sons—
          6 attache cases, 16 in., at £1·25 each.
          6 attache cases, 14 in., at £1·15 each.

     19. Bought from T. Jones & Sons—
          1 doz. gentlemen's umbrellas, hook handles, Union covers, at £1·75 each.

     21. Bought from Jardin & Sons—
          6 ladies' handbags, dark blue morocco, at £2·05 each.
          6 ladies' handbags, red morocco, at £1·75 each.

EXERCISE 84

From the following transactions write up the Sales Journal of Thomas Sheldon & Sons, warehousemen, whose business is in three departments, viz., Hosiery, Hats, and Trimmings—

July 1. Sold to Miriam, Ltd.—
          6 doz. pairs Rayon hose, point heels, assorted sizes and shades, at £6·50 per doz. pairs.

      5. Sold to T. Platt & Co.—
          3 doz. straws at £3·30 per doz.

      7. Sold to Jones & Morgan—
          5 doz. assorted feather trimmings in boxes, Nos. 491 to 494 and 497, at £3·25 per doz.

ADDITIONAL EXERCISES
Graded Book-keeping Exercises, Nos. 137 to 141.

CHAPTER XXVI

BANK RECONCILIATION STATEMENTS

WHENEVER money is paid into the bank, the Bank Account is debited and whenever money is drawn out the account is credited. A debit balance in the Bank Account indicates that money is owing *by* the bank: a credit balance that the account is overdrawn, that money is owing *to* the bank.

In the bank's books the position will be reversed: money paid in will be *credited* to the customer and money paid out will be debited. A *credit* balance on the account will indicate money due to the customer: a debit balance will indicate that he has an overdraft.

Periodically, at intervals agreed with the customer, the bank will send a Statement giving details of the account since the last Statement was issued. The Statement is a copy of the customer's account in the bank's Ledger.

On receipt of the Statement, the business will check the debit (or credit) balance as shown by the Cash Book with the credit (or debit) balance as shown by the Statement. These should agree in theory but it seldom happens in business practice that they do. The difference will not be due necessarily to errors in either account, but in order to be certain that there are no errors, all amounts are carefully checked. The items on the *debit* side of the Cash Book are checked against items on the *credit* side of the Statement: the items on the *credit* side of the Cash Book against those on the *debit* side of the Statement. All items which agree are ticked.

There are, therefore, four groups of possible differences which will consist of the four sets of unticked items in the four columns of the two accounts. These differences are reconciled in the Bank Reconciliation Statement which is a memorandum statement (i.e. not part of the double-entry system) made generally in the Cash Book just after the balance.

1. Items unticked on the *debit* side of the Cash Book will probably be sums of money paid into the bank at a branch other than the one at which the account is kept. There may be a few days' delay between the time such sums are paid in and the date on which the account of the business is credited by the bank. Thus credits paid into other bank branches within the last few days may have *not yet been credited*.

2. Items unticked on the *credit* side of the Cash Book (the most numerous) will be cheques paid out, again in the last day or so, but which have *not yet been presented* to our bank for payment. As our bank know nothing about these cheques until they are presented they cannot debit our account in their books. The debits are made in the following week or so as the cheques are presented.

3. Items unticked in the *debit* column of the Bank Statement are standing orders and charges which the bank debit to its customer's accounts without sending advices. The customer is first aware that the charge has been made when he reviews his Bank Statement. A credit for these items will have to be made in the Cash Book in the next period.

4. Items unticked in the *credit* column of the Bank Statement are very rare. They are items which have been added to the customer's account without his being advised, an example being Interest on Deposit Account. The debit entries must be made in the Cash Book during the next period.

The following worked example shows items ticked in the Bank Statement and the Cash Book and the Bank Reconciliation Statement made up from the *unticked* items in both. In the Reconciliation Statement shown, the first item is "Balance as per Cash Book," but it is possible to start with "Balance as per Statement." The important thing to remember is that whichever balance is started with, the differences must be added and/or subtracted to arrive at the other balance. Failure to secure this agreement means that there must be an arithmetical error in the Statement or the Cash Book.

The following transactions appeared in the Bank columns of V. Redman's Cash Book for the month of July.

Example

CASH BOOK (BANK COLUMNS ONLY)

19..			£	19..			£
July 1	Balance .	b/d	217·00	July 1	Petty Cash .		10·00√
4	J. Venner .		91·00√	2	B. Smithers .		18·60√
9	Cash Sales .		44·50√	4	Drawings .		20·00√
10	S. Jameson .		84·00√	5	Wages . .		12·00√
17	D.V.&Co.			9	T. Timpson .		72·00√
	Ltd. .		77·00√	12	Wages . .		12·00√
20	Cash Sales .		73·23√	19	Wages . .		12·00√
29	P. Johns,			26	S. Taylor .		35·24
	Ltd. .		16·00√		Wages . .		12·00√
31	B. Benskin .		229·55	30	M. Nunns .		4·00
					B. Western		48·00
				31	Balance .	c/d	576·44
			£832·28				£832·28
Aug. 1	Balance	b/d	576·44				

Note that as it is customary in bank accounting to balance *daily*, the balance shown in the following Statement is cumulative. The last figure in the right-hand column is the balance at the end of the month.

BANK STATEMENT

Date	Details	Debit	Credit	Balance
July 1	Balance			217·00
	Cash	10·00√		207·00
4	Cash	20·00√		187·00
	Cheque	18·60√		168·40
5	Cheque		91·00√	259·40
	Cash—wages	12·00√		247·40
9	Cash		44·50√	291·90
11	Cheque		84·00√	375·90
12	Cash—wages	12·00√		363·90
	Cheque book	0·42		363·48
19	Cheque		77·00√	
	Cheque—wages	12·00√		428·48
20	Cheque	72·00√		356·48
	Cash		73·23√	429·71
26	Cash	12·00√		417·71
30	Investment Co., Ltd. . . .		10·50	
	Cheque Due		16·00√	444·21

BANK RECONCILIATION STATEMENT
AS AT 31ST JULY, 19..

	£	£	£
Balance as per Cash Book			576·44
Add cheques not yet presented—			
S. Taylor	35·24		
M. Nunns	4·00		
B. Western	48·00		
		87·24	
Add amount paid direct—Investment Co., Ltd. .		10·50	
			97·74
			674·18
Less payment in not yet credited—			
B. Benskin	229·55		
Less Cheque book	0·42		
			229·97
Balance as per Bank Statement			£444·21

EXERCISE 85

The Bank columns in S. James's Cash Book for the month of February were as follows—

19..				£	19..				£
Feb. 1	Balance .	b/d	320·00		Feb. 5	L. Langridge	.		100·00
9	B. Jones .	.	70·00		10	K. Glickston	.		160·00
15	M. Shales .	.	140·00		17	M. Barrass .	.		20·00
27	C. Dingle .	.	250·00		26	J. Blake .	.		110·00
28	S. Paul .	.	75·00			R. Joyce .	.		70·00
					28	S. Beamish .	.		40·00
						Balance	.	c/d	355·00
			£855·00						£855·00
Mar. 1	Balance	b/d	355·00						

His Bank Statement made up to the end of February was as follows—

Date	Details	Debit	Credit	Balance
19..		£	£	£
Feb. 1	Balance brought forward .			320·00
8	Cheque—L. Langridge . . .	100·00		220·00
11	Cheque		70·00	290·00
	Cheque—K. Glickston . . .	160·00		130·00
17	Cheque		140·00	27·000
18	Cheque—M. Barrass . . .	20·00		250·00
28	Cheque—R. Joyce . . .	70·00		180·00
	Cheque—J. Blake	110·00		70·00

You are required to prepare a Statement reconciling the balances at 28th February.

EXERCISE 86

The Bank columns in the Cash Book of V. Wisdom showed that the following transactions had taken place in the month of September—

19..			£	19..			£
Sept. 1	Balance . .	b/d	640·00	Sept. 4	S. Richards .		40·00
3	Sales . .		130·00	7	Wages .		110·00
7	W. Brixham .		44·00	8	S. Knutson .		62·00
13	Z. Austin . .		76·00	11	B. Wills . .		68·00
19	S. Michum .		236·00	14	Petty Cash .		10·00
23	Smith & Jones .		81·00	17	J. Todd . .		98·00
27	Ball, Ltd. .		101·00	21	Wages . .		112·00
30	Granger & Co. .		315·00	29	W. Gilbey .		75·00
				30	S. Wolfson .		136·00
					J. Petter .		28·00
					Balance .	c/d	884·00
			£1,623·00				£1,623·00
Oct. 1	Balance . .	b/d	884·00				

The Bank's record of Wisdom's account showed as follows—

Date	Details	Debit	Credit	Balance
19..		£	£	£
Sept. 1	Balance brought forward . .			640·00
3	Cash		130·00	770·00
7	Cash—Wages . . .	110·00		660·00
9	Cheque		44·00	704·00
10	Cheque—S. Richards . .	40·00		664·00
12	Cheque—B. Wills . .	68·00		
	Cheque—S. Knutson .	62·00		534·00
14	Cash	10·00		524·00
	Cheque . . .		76·00	600·00
16	Cheque Book . . .	0·42		599·58
20	Cheque		236·00	835·58
21	Cheque—J. Todd . .	98·00		737·58
	Cash—Wages . .	112·00		625·58
22	Charges . . .	1·58		624·00
24	Cheque		81·00	705·00
30	Cheque		101·00	806·00

ADDITIONAL EXERCISES

Graded Book-keeping Exercises, Nos. 142 to 148.

CHAPTER XXVII

SINGLE-ENTRY

THE system of double-entry book-keeping is based on the principle that every transaction involving money or money's worth may be viewed from two aspects, and that the recording of two aspects of a transaction in accounts involves a debit and a credit entry.

Single-entry book-keeping is the name given in practice to all forms of book-keeping which do not comply with the basic rules of the double-entry system. In many cases the two-fold aspect of a few transactions will be recorded, but the principle is not adhered to consistently. Apart from the Cash Book, which is usually kept, the single-entry "system" is a record of the personal aspect of transactions only. Generally it will be found that the books consist of a Cash Book, often a Ledger or Ledgers for the accounts of customers, and possibly a Sales Journal, and, less likely, a Bought Journal. The personal accounts of customers may be posted from a Sales Journal, but the credit entry for sales will not be made, and, apart from the posting to the customers' accounts, no further use will be made of the Sales Journal entries. Purchases may be recorded in a Bought Journal and posted therefrom to the credit of the respective personal accounts, or the entry may be made direct to the Ledger from the invoices received. Cash dealings will be entered in the Cash Book and posted to the personal accounts, but, usually, capital in cash, drawings, expenses, and the purchase of assets will be recorded only in the Cash Book, no real or nominal accounts being found in the Ledger.

Such a record has obvious disadvantages when compared with the double-entry system. For example, under single-entry book-keeping—

162

It is impossible to extract a Trial Balance to prove the arithmetical accuracy of the Ledger.

As no real or property accounts are kept, it is impossible to ascertain from the Ledger any information respecting the assets of the business, their present value, and whether due allowance has been made for wastage or depreciation.

As no nominal accounts are kept, no information is readily available respecting the gains or losses of the business, either for use in ascertaining the present position of affairs or for comparison with previous years in an attempt to locate causes of decline or increase in profits.

The record is incomplete for the purpose of ascertaining the profits for a trading period, and usually much of the information has to be obtained from other sources.

Profit or Loss under Single-entry

To discover the results of trading it is necessary to find the capital of the business as at the close of the trading period, and to compare it with the capital as at the commencement of the period. If the capital at the close is greater than the capital at the beginning the difference is regarded as profit. A loss is indicated if the capital at the close is less than the capital at the start of the trading period. The capital, of course, in both cases equals the excess of assets over liabilities. Allowance must be made, as shown later, for any drawings during the year.

To ascertain the financial position at any time a Statement of Affairs is drawn up. If the capital at the start is not known, a similar statement must be prepared as at the commencement of the period. The information required is—

1. The total of debtors and creditors as shown by the personal accounts in the Ledger.
2. The cash in hand and the bank balance.
3. Stock in hand duly valued.
4. All assets noted and their present values ascertained.
5. Outstanding expenses and payments in advance.

This information is set out in the Statement of Affairs, the assets on the right-hand side and the liabilities on the left-hand side, the difference between the two sides representing the capital or deficiency of capital as the case may be. The insertion of this difference on the appropriate side balances the statement.

The excess of the capital shown by the Statement of Affairs as at the close of the trading period over the capital as at the beginning of the period represents the profits which have been made.

Account must be taken, however, in calculating the profit, of any drawings during the year and of any capital added or withdrawn. The drawings made (in cash or kind) must be added to the closing capital. Additions to capital during the year must be deducted. Withdrawal of capital must be added. Only after such adjustments should the difference between the amount of the opening and the closing capitals be ascertained.

Example

A manufacturer, Philip Morgan, kept his books on what is known as the single-entry system. The position of the business at 31st December, 19.., revealed the following—

					£
Freehold Premises	.	.	.	.	1,000
Plant and Machinery	.	.	.	.	600
Stock-in-trade	.	.	.	.	1,300
Sundry Debtors	.	.	.	.	1,750
Cash at Bank	.	.	.	.	300
Sundry Creditors	.	.	.	.	1,875

At 1st January of that year his capital was £5,500. During the year his drawings amounted to £500, and the sale of his private motor-car realized £200, which he paid into the bank to the credit of the business current account.

You are required to prepare the Statement of Affairs showing the financial position of Philip Morgan as at 31st December, compile his Capital Account at that date, and ascertain the amount of his profit or loss of the year.

(R.S.A.)

STATEMENT OF AFFAIRS

31st December, 19..

	£		£
Sundry Creditors . .	1,875	Freehold Premises . .	1,000
Capital . . .	3,075	Plant and Machinery .	600
		Stock . . .	1,300
		Sundry Debtors . .	1,750
		Cash at Bank . .	300
	£4,950		£4,950

(*Note.* The Capital, £3,075, is the difference between the two sides.)

STATEMENT OF PROFIT OR LOSS
FOR THE YEAR

	£
Capital (31st December)	3,075
Add Drawings	500
	3,575
Deduct cash paid in	200
	£3,375

	£
Capital (1st January)	5,500
Less Adjusted Capital (31st December)	3,375
Net loss .	£2,125

Dr.				CAPITAL—PHILIP MORGAN				Cr.
19..			£	19..				£
Dec. 31	Drawings . .		500	Jan. 1	Balance . .			5,500
	Net loss . .		2,125	Dec. 31	Cash . . .			200
	Balance . .	c/d	3,075					
			£5,700					£5,700
				Jan. 1	Balance .	b/d		3,075

Conversion of Single-entry to Double-entry

The preparation of a Statement of Affairs enables a start to be made to convert the books to the double-entry system. The items in the Statement of Affairs provide the information for the opening entries in the Journal from which the assets and liabilities will be posted to the appropriate accounts. It will be necessary to open new accounts where they do not already exist as, for instance, for the various assets.

The next step will be to analyse the items for the trading period, and to ensure that the double-entry is completed for items already entered on one side of the accounts, and the full double-entry is made for items not entered at all.

The purchases must be analysed and the Purchases Account posted. Purchases of fixed assets and consumable material (stationery, etc.) must be posted to the appropriate real and expense accounts.

Similarly, the sales must be entered in the Sales Account, and due account taken of any purchases or sales returned by entries in the Purchases Returns Account and Sales Returns Account respectively. This should complete the double-entry for most of the items found in the personal accounts. Such items as remain will consist of entries for allowances, bad debts written off, and the double-entry should be completed, also, for all these.

The Cash Book must be scrutinized so that all unposted items are taken to their appropriate accounts. These will consist of expenses paid such as rent, insurance, wages, and cash purchases and sales. The discount columns of the Cash Book, if any, will require to be totalled and transferred to the Discount Accounts. If no discount is shown, then the necessary entries must be obtained by examination of the personal accounts.

Any further one-sided entries that remain should be posted to their respective accounts, and the double-entry for all the transactions should then be complete.

The extraction of a Trial Balance should prove the clerical

accuracy of the accounts, and the books are now ready for closing and the preparation of the final accounts.

The above has reference to the conversion of the single-entry record of a year's working to double-entry principle. It may be, however, that the intention is to keep the books, *in future*, on the double-entry system. Then the Statement of Affairs as at the *close* of the trading period will provide the opening entries for the Journal from which the new set of books will be posted, and all transactions in the future will be recorded in the usual subsidiary books and posted to the Ledger on the double-entry principles.

Trading and Profit and Loss Accounts in Single-entry

Sometimes a trader who is unable, or unprepared, to operate a full system of double-entry book-keeping is anxious to have more details of how his profit is made up then he can obtain from the very sketchy information available in his Statement of Profit.

It is possible to give him a Trading and Profit and Loss Account if he, as a minimum requirement, will keep a properly detailed Cash Book showing exactly what money was received for and exactly how money was spent. This Cash Book must be summarized at the end of the trading period, and, in conjunction with the opening and closing Statements of Affairs, will give the required information.

What happens can best be illustrated by the following example.

Example

T. Briggs' summarized Cash Book for the year ended 31st March, 19.., was as follows—

CASH BOOK

(Summary)

		£			£
Balance .	b/f	200	Salaries and Wages		650
Cash Sales .		3,000	Heat and Light .		80
Cash received			Carriage on Sales .		40
from Debtors .		4,500	Carriage on		
			Purchases . .		60
			Insurance . .		30
			Cash Purchases .		1,000
			Cash paid to		
			Creditors . .		3,200
			General Expenses .		500
			Additional		
			Machinery .		1,000
			Drawings . .		800
			Balance .	c/d	340
		£7,700			£7,700
Balance .	b/d	340			

His Statement of Affairs at the beginning of the year was—

STATEMENT OF AFFAIRS OF T. BRIGGS

AS AT 31ST MARCH, 19..

	£		£
Capital	8,000	FIXED ASSETS	
Sundry Creditors . .	1,150	Land and Buildings .	4,000
		Plant and Machinery .	2,000
		CURRENT ASSETS	
		Stock	2,500
		Sundry Debtors . .	450
		Cash	200
	£9,150		£9,150

From the foregoing and the information given below prepare a Trading and Profit and Loss Account for the year for Briggs, and his closing Statement of Affairs. At the end of the year his financial position was: Cash, £340; Stock, £3,000; Sundry Debtors, £400; Land and Buildings, £4,000; Plant and Machinery, £2,000 (plus additions as shown in Cash Book); Sundry Creditors, £1,250. During the year he had drawn £800 on account of profits. Of the amount spent on Insurance £10 refers to the next trading period. The old balance of Plant and Machinery is to be depreciated by 10 per cent.

The only difficulty a student should meet in producing the Trading Account is in discovering the amount of credit sales and purchases for the year, since no records are kept other than those given here. These amounts can be found thus—

	£		£
Take the *closing* figure for Debtors	400	and Creditors . . .	1,250
Add amount received from Debtors	4,500	and paid to Creditors . .	3,200
	4,900		4,450
Deduct opening figure for Debtors	450	and Creditors . . .	1,150
Total amount sold on credit for year	4,450	bought on Credit . .	3,300
Add Cash Sales . . .	3,000	Cash Purchases . .	1,000
Total Sales and Purchases for year	£7,450		£4,300

The Trading and Profit and Loss Account can now be done. It will appear as follows—

TRADING AND PROFIT AND LOSS ACCOUNT OF T. BRIGGS
FOR THE YEAR ENDED 31ST MARCH, 19..

	£		£
Stock . . .	2,500	Sales	7,450
Purchases . . .	4,300	Stock	3,000
Carriage on Purchases .	60		
Gross Profit c/d . .	3,590		
	£10,450		£10,450
Salaries and Wages . .	650	Gross Profit b/d . .	3,590
Heating and Lighting . .	80		
Carriage on Sales . .	40		
Insurance . . £30			
Less in advance . 10			
	20		
General Expenses . .	500		
Depreciation—			
Machinery . . .	200		
Net Profit transferred to Capital . . .	2,100		
	£3,590		£3,590

Briggs' closing Statement would appear thus—

STATEMENT OF AFFAIRS OF T. BRIGGS
AS AT 31ST MARCH, 19..

	£	£			£	£
Capital . . .	8,000		FIXED ASSETS—			
Add Net Profit . .	2,100		Land and Buildings .			4,000
	10,100		Plant and			
Less Drawings . .	800		Machinery £2,000			
		9,300	*Less* 10%			
Sundry Creditors . .		1,250	Depreciation 200		1,800	
			Add purchases			
			during year . .		1,000	
						2, 00
			CURRENT ASSETS—			
			Stock . .			3,000
			Sundry Debtors .			400
			Cash . .			340
			Insurance in advance			10
		£10,550				£10,550

EXERCISE 87

Wilson had not kept his books on the double-entry system. He started trading on 1st January with a capital of £5,000 cash in the bank. During the year he drew for private use £600.

His position at 31st December was given as follows—

	£
Freehold Premises	1,200
Plant	500
Fittings	200
Stock	1,500
Debtors	1,500
Creditors	1,750
Cash at Bank	500

Prepare a suitable statement showing Wilson's financial position on 31st December and the profit or loss for the year.

EXERCISE 88

E. Bateman started business on 1st January, 19.., with cash £2,000, which he paid into a banking account, and stock valued at £2,000.

At the end of the year the following particulars were supplied—

	£
Debtors	2,500
Stock	2,400
Furniture and Fixtures	300
Creditors	1,800
Motor Van	200
Cash	600

His drawings during the year amounted to £640.

Prepare a statement showing Bateman's profit or loss on the year's working

EXERCISE 89

The following "Statements of Affairs" have been drawn up to give the financial position, as on 31st March, 19.., and the following 31st March respectively, of A. Brown, who keeps his books on a single-entry basis—

STATEMENT OF AFFAIRS, 31st March, 19..

	£			£
Capital	6,192	Fixtures		250
Creditors . . .	742	Stock . . .		2,305
		Debtors . . .		4,176
		Cash		203
	£6,934			£6,934

STATEMENT OF AFFAIRS, 31st March, 19..

	£			£
Capital	5,933	Fixtures . . .		230
Creditors . . .	817	Stock . . .		2,562
		Debtors . . .		3,777
		Cash . . .		181
	£6,750			£6,750

Brown has transferred £100 a month regularly from his business banking account to his private banking account by way of drawings, and he has taken £25 worth of stock for his private use. The alteration in the value of the fixtures represents an amount written off by way of depreciation.

Calculate Brown's trading profit for the year.   (R.S.A.)

EXERCISE 90

B. Gurles and C. Boyes were partners in a toy manufacturing business sharing profits and losses equally, the capital also belonging to them in equal shares. On 1st July, 19.., their financial position was as follows—

	£	£		£
Capital—			Cash in hand . . .	20
B. Gurles . .	6,000		Sundry Debtors .	5,100
C. Boyes . .	6,000		Stock in trade . .	3,380
		12,000	Plant and Machinery .	6,250
Sundry Creditors .		2,500	Fixtures, Fittings, etc. .	250
Bank Overdraft .		500		
		£15,000		£15,000

They had not kept proper books on the double-entry system but ask you to ascertain whether they have made a profit or a loss for the year ended 30th June, 19.., and upon investigation you obtain the following particulars as at 30th June, 19..: Cash in hand, £25; Sundry Debtors, £5,420; Stock in Trade, £3,750; Sundry Creditors, £2,490; Bank Overdraft, £150. During the year each of the partners had drawn £350. It was agreed that a provision of £120 should be made for Bad Debts, and that £250 should be written off Plant and Machinery and 10 per cent off Fixtures and Fittings. Each partner is entitled to interest at 5 per cent per annum on his capital.

Set out the statements which you would present to the partners.

(U.L.C.I.)

ADDITIONAL EXERCISES

Graded Book-keeping Exercises, Nos. 202 to 204.

CHAPTER XXVIII

CAPITAL AND REVENUE EXPENDITURE: ACCOUNTS OF NON-TRADING ORGANIZATIONS

THE importance of being able to appreciate the nature of different items of expenditure cannot be over-stressed when preparing accounts that are intended to give an accurate picture of the financial affairs of a concern.

Capital and Revenue Expenditure

In Chapter VI the different kinds of Purchases a business makes were discussed. Briefly they can be summarized as—

(a) Money spent on the purchase of fixed assets.

(b) Money spent on the purchase of goods for resale.

(c) Money spent on the purchase of goods and services to be consumed in the furtherance of business activities.

Group (a) can be regarded as *permanent* purchases, that is, the purchases (land, machinery, furniture, etc.) will be retained in the business, for many years perhaps. Such purchases are regarded as *Capital Expenditure*.

Groups (b) and (c) are not bought to be retained and are known as *Revenue Expenditure*.

Naturally, what will be regarded as capital and what as revenue expenditure will vary from business to business. For instance, a trader in office equipment who buys a typewriter for sale to a customer will regard the purchase as revenue expenditure: any other business house buying a typewriter will do so for use in its office and will correctly regard such a purchase as capital expenditure.

Most expenditure is easily classified as either capital or revenue, but some items cause difficulty. For example, if a business expended £500 on new parts for some machinery, is the amount to be regarded as capital expenditure, which means the £500 is added to the book value of the asset, or is it to be regarded as revenue expenditure, which means the book value goes unaltered and the £500 is written off against profit? Of course, only a knowledge of the particular circumstances will decide this, as in all cases where there is doubt. It will be evident that the distinction between the two kinds of expenditure is important since the one reduces the profit while the other increases the fixed assets.

Accounts on Non-trading Organizations

It is necessary that dramatic societies, tennis clubs and other like social organizations, as well as the many institutions founded for a variety of purposes, should all keep accounts. They depend for their income not on the sale of goods or services, but on subscriptions and donations of members and others. They can be regarded as having made a profit if their revenue income for a particular period exceeded their revenue expenditure for that period, but such "profit" is not distributed to the members but is retained in the organization, to further the cause for which it was founded. These remarks apply to "profit" made on any fund-raising ventures such as whist-drives, dances, jumble sales, etc.

The accounts of non-trading organizations can be kept on the double-entry system, but with two important differences from accounts of trading or profit-making organizations—

1. There is no Capital Account indicating money put in and withdrawable by an owner or owners. Monies received are debited to Cash (or Bank) Account and credited to the Income and Expenditure Account (see below) or to a Consolidated Fund or some similarly named account the equivalent of the Capital Account.

2. Final Accounts, prepared periodically as desired, will consist of a Receipts and Payments Account, an Income and Expenditure Account and a Balance Sheet. Copies of these are presented to the members.

The Receipts and Payments Account

This is a summary of the Cash Account and shows: (a) the opening Cash Balance; (b) all monies received during the period (whether referring to that period or not, e.g. subscriptions received in advance refer to the next period); (c) all monies paid out during the period (whether referring to that period or not); and (d) the closing cash balance.

The Income and Expenditure Account

This is easier to understand if it is thought of as a species of Profit and Loss Account. All items of revenue expenditure for that period (whether paid in the previous or some subsequent period) are debited. All items of revenue income which belong to that period (whether received in that period or not) are credited. The excess of income over expenditure (a "profit") is credited to the Consolidated Fund Account: the excess of expenditure over income (a "loss") is debited to the Consolidated Fund Account.

The Balance Sheet

This will appear as usual. The debit side will show fixed and current Assets and payments in advance, though sometimes the order is reversed and assets are placed in order of realizability, with cash first.

The credit side will show the balance of the consolidated fund with the "profit" added or "loss" deducted; any loans; sundry creditors; and payments in arrears or accrued due.

The following simple worked example is given to assist the student.

Example

The Circle Athletic Club was formed on 1st May, 19.., with a membership of 50. The 30 adult members pay 25p per month: the 20 junior members pay 20p per month.

From the following summary extracted from the club's records prepare the Receipts and Payments Account, the Income and Expenditure Account, and the Balance Sheet as at 31st May.

(i) Subscriptions were received for the month from 28 adult members, of whom 6 paid in advance for the next month. All junior members paid up.

(ii) A raffle to raise funds cost £4. Receipts were £12·50.

(iii) A jumble sale was held. Costs £3·50. Receipts £16·50.

(iv) Printing, stationery, advertising, etc., £8·55.

(v) Hire of gymnasium, pitches, etc., from the local authority, £10.

(vi) Purchase of second-hand sports equipment, £12.

RECEIPTS AND PAYMENTS ACCOUNT OF THE CIRCLE ATHLETIC CLUB

FOR THE MONTH ENDED 31ST MAY, 19..

	£		£
Subscriptions received—		Expenses of Raffle . . .	4·00
28 Adult Members—May . .	7·00	Expenses of Jumble Sale .	3·50
6 Adult Members—June . .	1·50	Printing, Stationery, etc. .	8·55
20 Junior Members—May . .	4·00	Hire of Gymnasium, Pitches, .	
Receipts from Raffle . .	12·50	etc.	10.00
Receipts from Jumble Sale . .	16·50	Second-hand Sports Equip-	
		ment	12·00
		Balance of Cash c/f . .	3·45
	£41·50		£41·50

INCOME AND EXPENDITURE ACCOUNT OF THE CIRCLE ATHLETIC CLUB

FOR THE MONTH ENDED 31ST MAY, 19..

	£		£
Expenses of Raffle . .	4·00	Subscriptions Receivable—	
Expenses of Jumble Sale .	3·50	30 Adult Members @ £0·25	7·50
Printing, Stationery, etc. .	8·55	20 Junior Members @ £0·20	4·00
Hire of Gymnasium, etc. .	10·00	Receipts from Raffle . .	12·50
Excess of Income over Expendi-		Receipts from Jumble Sale .	16·50
ture to Balance Sheet . .	14·45		
	£40·50		£40·50

BALANCE SHEET OF THE CIRCLE ATHLETIC CLUB

AS AT 31ST MAY, 19..

Liabilities	£	Assets	£
Excess of Income over Ex-		Cash in hand . . .	3·45
penditure . . .	14·45	Subscriptions in arrears .	0·50
Subscriptions received in		Equipment . . .	12·00
advance . . .	1·50		
	£15·95		£15·95

EXERCISE 91

(a) Is it true that all expenditure which cannot be classified as capital expenditure *must* be classified as revenue expenditure? Give reasons for your answer.

(b) Make a list of capital expenditure and a list of revenue expenditure items which might be made by—

(i) A bakery.
(ii) A chimney sweep.
(iii) A chain store.

EXERCISE 92

The balances in the books of the Southern Cricket Club on 1st June were Cash at Bank, £406; Equipment, £210; Ground and Pavilion, £1,000; Consolidated Fund, £1,616. From this information and that given below prepare final accounts for the month of June for presentation to members.

(i) Subscriptions received £35, of which £3 is in advance; £10 was in arrears for the month.

(ii) Receipts from 2 matches, £30.

(iii) Expenses of players visiting other clubs, £15.

(iv) Upkeep of pavilion and ground—wages, etc., £45.

(v) Sundry expenses, £3·40.

(vi) Purchases of equipment, £10. Old balance of equipment to be depreciated by 5 per cent.

(Cash Balance, £397·60. Excess of expenditure over income, £1·90.
Balance Sheet totals, £1,617·10.)

ADDITIONAL EXERCISES

Graded Book-keeping Exercises, Nos. 205 to 210.

(Exercises in comprehension and interpretation of work covered in this volume can be found in *Graded Book-keeping Exercises*, Nos. 149 to 204.)

INDEX